# FLOWERS
# OF
# HINDU CHIVALRY

# FLOWERS OF HINDU CHIVALRY

HEM CHANDRA RAI

GYAN

*Published by*

GYAN

Gyan Publishing House
5, Ansari Road
Daryaganj, New Delhi-110002
Phone: 011-47034999, 9811692060
E-mail: books@gyanbooks.com

*Distribution Network*
gyanbooks.com
India, USA, Canada, UK, Australia



ISBN: 978-93-6780-381-3 (HB)

First Published, 1932

2nd Impression 2024

*Printed at:* Gyan Press, Delhi.



**FLOWERS OF HINDU CHIVALRY**
Author: HEM CHANDRA RAI

# FLOWERS
# OF
# HINDU CHIVALRY.

*By*

HEM CHANDRA RAI M. A.

Ex Senior State Secretary, Sirmoor State.
Author of "Romance of the Fort of Gwalior."
"Administrative Reform in Indian states."

*Foreword*

*By*

Lt. Colonel H. L. O. Garrett M. A., I. E. S.

*ILLUSTRATED*

1932

# CONTENTS.

# LIST OF ILLUSTRATIONS.

# FOREWORD.

I have been asked by my old pupil, Mr. H. C. Rai, to write a brief Foreword to his series of studies of the Hindu Chivalry of India. It is some years since something of the sort was attempted in "When Kings rode to Delhi" but the larger portion of that work is concerned with the Mughals and their predecessors. The present volume therefore fills a gap for there is no doubt that a study of the great deeds of his fellow countrymen in the past should from part of the education of every good citizen. As the author points out, most English lads owe much to Henty and other similar authors, who have concentrated upon the great characters of the past, and the Indian lad of today cannot but benefit from a study of the deeds of the mirrors of chivalry of a bygone day. Every nation can do with a Froissart and the author is attempting something of the sort in India.

H. L. O. GARRETT M. A., I. E. S.,
Principal, Government College,

JANUARY 1932. LAHORE.

# FOREWORD

[illegible]

# PROLOGUE.

"Oh, who shall lightly say that fame
Is but an empty name
Whilst in that sound there is a charm
The nerve to brace, the heart to warm,
As thinking of the mighty dead,
The young from youthful couch will start.
And vow with lifted hands outspread,
Like them to act a noble part."

*Joanna Baillie.*

Over the rugged road of History, broken with the rises and falls of nations, the Hindus have steadily marched from times immemorial, braving frequent storms of varying intensity and duration which would have annihilated a people of lesser genius. The process of evolution of Hindu destiny through the ages gone by is a vast study in itself. Seething with life and high impulses, the Hindus are to-day a nation richly endowed with a glorious civilization, mental culture, martial traditions and all those virtues which entitle them to be reckoned among the living nations of the modern world. The genius of our numerous race has not deteriorated in the smallest degree; nor are our potentialities small for the future. We have had periods of doubt and depression in our chequered national existence but the nation has sprung up phoenix-like from its ashes time after time, shaking itself free from past political immoralities and mistakes. The poet truly says—

"The forces of decay build life anew
For the next onward sweep to gain a height;
The free life stirs, if it be free and true;
Graves are our footholds for the forward fight."

About a thousand years ago the Hindus felt the first shock of Islam but were hardly awakened from the morbid spell which spiritual life had apparently cast over them. A multiplicity of spiritual preceptors taught the people to subordinate the desire for material advancement to spiritual uplift. However the ideal was degenerated in practice to such an extent that the Hindus lost their hold on the philosophy of action; on the contrary their aspirations and efforts were centred round the life after death, in which they devoutly believed. The mental outlook of the masses was so completely metamorphosed in course of time that renunciation came to be looked upon as a positive merit, heedless of the fact that this strained attitude was beginning to jeopardise the political interests of the nation. The average Hindu cared more to earn religious merit by practising penance and renunciation in this earthly existence than to live a full measure of his *life*, battling his way bravely through it, developing his material advantages and manfully doing his duties towards the State. Whether the Hindu sages of antiquity foresaw the danger of political degeneracy which mass religiosity in an aggravated form, with an overwhelming craving for realms of the spirit, might produce, is difficult to say. A clear index of the mass mind, labouring under a false sense of religious obsession, is furnished by the attitude displayed by Arjun at the outbreak of the war of the Mahabharat. As soon as the gallant Arjun witnessed his own kinsmen arrayed in battle against him, his mighty frame and lofty courage were numbed into inactivity by thoughts of the destructive selfishness of human ambitions. Actuated by feelings of disgust, he laid down his arms on the battlefield and resolved to retire when the omniscience of Lord Krishna revealed to Him the faltering soul of the celebrated warrior. Then the Lord treated Arjun to that divine discourse on the philosophy of action known as the holy Gita, which not only dispelled his gloomy reflections and impelled him into instantaneous action, but has for thousands of years shone as the immortal refutation of the cult of cowardice and cant. What a dream of fighting odours is awakened by the Gita and all that it has done to inspire the Hindu race in the past !

## IV

Some of the bravest Hindus have been devout votaries of the Gita, which furnishes a splendid mould for Hindu character and conduct. Due to disregard of its sublime teachings, our corporate existence has not only been starved of its natural scope for development but it has been driven into narrow limits out of which repeated attempts have been made to wriggle out.

A more important factor which has imposed a terrible brake on the progress of the race is the institution of castes. It was never intended by the ancient law-givers that Hindu society should be dissected into four parts, or castes, in which the higher ones should exult in their inheritance of social superiority irrespective of individual merit or fitness. In short caste came to be wantonly degraded into a system of grave social wrong based on the pure accident of birth. The Kshattriyas were exclusively saddled with the burden of fighting the battles of Hinduism. The rigidity of caste eliminated the possibility of making good the loss of numbers which ensued among them in Northern India when the countless hordes of Islam swept down from the North West in whirlwinds of religious frenzy. While caste in its vulgar from served to turn out the Kshattriyas more and more into specialists for war, which is the one useful purpose it did serve, it unfortunately strangled the martial potentialities of the other three Hindu castes, who found it convenient to shift the dangerous duties of war on other's shoulders under the solemn sanction of selfish pedagogues who did not scruple to prostitute their garb of religion for ulterior motives. For how can any thoughtful human being ever admit for a moment that millions of healthy able-bodied men and their countless progeny, to be born in after ages, could be reasonably declared unfit for the pursuit of war and its kindred duties by some religious dictum ? The very idea is monstrous, unnatural and altogether suicidal from the political point of view. The inevitable consequence of the practice of caste by birth was that a marked physical deterioration set in among the three non-military castes, who knowing themselves to be destined to follow civil avocations, cared little for physical development and less for proficiency in the use of arms. The Mahomedan invaders found the millions of Hindus belonging to these castes as tame as herds of cattle and drove them as such before them after the resistance offered by the military caste was overcome. The Kshattriyas were ill-prepared to resist the ceaseless deluge of invasion, which bore down all before it, obliterating ancient land-marks, wiping out dynasties and decimating the valiant Kshattriyas who were frequently outnumbered in the portentous and protracted struggle. Not only were the Kshattriyas heavily handicapped in war by the dead weight of the overwhelming majority of their own impotent co-religionists but they suffered even in a larger degree from lack of cohesion among themselves.

The Rajputs, as the Ksahattriyas were popularly called at the time of the Mahomedan conquest, were divided into numerous clans and were conservative by heredity. There was little love lost between the various clans and their feuds were kept alive by intermittent orgies of blood, which caused mortal injury to the national interests. Like the old Highland clans of Scotland, the Rajput clans could never hold together for long except under extraordinary compulsion and even then for short periods. The country was split up into hundreds of petty Rajput principalities, whose chiefs seldom cared to combine even when faced by a common danger. This disruptive state of affairs continued even after the Mahomedan conquest was an accomplished fact. Colonel Tod has borne eloquent testimony to the fact that had the three great ruling dynasties of Amber, Marwar and Mewar had the political sagacity to sink their mutual jealousies and unite, to wage a vigorous war against the Mogals, they could have thoroughly overpowered the empire of Delhi on several critical junctures in its history. Divide et impera is an old and favourite maxim of prudent rulers. The various Mahomedan dynasts of Delhi were fully aware of the deadly frailty of the Rajputs and never failed to exploit it to advance their political interests.

Akbar was gifted by nature with a nobler genius than his predecessors and with unerring judgment he determined to win over the brave Rajputs by genial persuasion snd generous treatment. His manliness, chivalry and even-handed justice were the traits which struck concordant notes in the Rajput character and excited their unstinted admiration. Where the politic emperor erred however was in forcing the dishonourable issue, viz vassalage, on Maharana Pratap Singh, the noblest patriot of Rajasthan. It was a political blunder which jarred on the fruition of the emperor's Rajput policy and focussed the unpleasant light of Hindu opinion on the vassalage of the other Rajput leaders. Pratap, the immortal patriot, had risen to a truer sense of patriotism and contempt for dependence than any other Rajput of his age. It is probable that after Pratap had driven the Mogals out of Mewar, Akbar refrained from seriously undertaking a second campaign against him for fear of the dire political consequences of another failure which must have dangerously augmented the great martial reputation, armed strength and resources of the Maharana. The Hindus at large were contented under Akbar's benevolent rule in Northern India. Lower down in the Deccan however a martial though unobtrusive evolution of Hindu society was proceeding apace in the interminable wars between the. independent Deccan kingdoms.

Before long Aurangzeb came to rule over the destinies of the Mogal empire and worked his batteries so zealously against the tolerant and sound statesmanship of his forbears as to demolish the great edifice of empire in a huge ruin. His policy of relentless repression and persecution of the Hindus wrought a cataclysmic change among them. Some of the greatest Hindu men-of-action sprang forth to champion the cause of their national culture, liberties and religion, which had been placed in grave jeopardy. The Rajputs awoke to the reality of the common menace and resolved to be no longer made the dupes and victims of unscrupulous imperial designs. In fact Rajasthan was scarred with the ruins which the Mogal legions left in their wake after the war of independence, in which Mewar and Marwar played so memorable a part. That the heart of the Hindu nation beat sound is amply proved by the fact that they began to fret under the hateful yoke and widely planned to overthrow it. Little fires quietly kindled in distant corners during the dark days of religious persecution soon spread and blazed out. Aurangzeb tried to extinguish them by torrents of blood but failed so signally that the fires developed into a terrific conflagration which consumed the empire itself. A number of venerable Hindu saints like Samarth Ram Das, Tuka Ram, and Prabhu Pran Nath aroused the soul of the people and infused them with the ardent craving to fight down tyrrany and wrong. Not one of the Hindu war captains of that epic age was a blind force. Each had keenly comprehended contemporary conditions, strove to unify them in himself and gave them a final irresistible impulsion.

The Marathas deserve the foremost place of honour in the powerful Hindu Renaissance which followed the debacle of the Mogal legions in the Deccan in the closing years of Aurangzeb's life. Quickenings of the new life had begun to be manifest soon after imperial tyranny reigned over the land but by the close of the 17th century it had gathered sufficient weight and momentum to batter down the weary, spiritless and exhausted empire of Delhi. That the political genius of the Marathas holds high rank in Hindu minds is unquestionably due to the fact that Maratha patriots went far to liberate the Hindu spirit from the thraldom of sectarian bigotry, which naturally led to the expansion of Hindu enterprise and achievement. Maratha banners symbolised the cooperation of the Hindu warrior races just as Prussia had carved out the unity of the numerous German states after the war of 1866 under the direction of Bismark. Although the Peshwas had usurped the power of the Maratha king as completely as the Shoguns had relegated the Mikado in Japan to a shadowy unconsidered figure in his ancestral palace at Kioto, yet this revolutionary change cast a beneficent influence on Hindu politics not only because it introduced a democratic element in the exercise of government but owing to the selfless and progressive outlook of the earlier Peshwas. The disaster at Panipat in 1761 proved to be only a temporary set back to the Maratha Commonwealth. It was soon retrieved and the orbits of sway of the Maratha war lords were again expanding till the close of the 18th century, when they found themselves pitched against the rising ambitions and power of Britain. Eventually victory shone on the banners of Britain; but it was not altogether a repetition of the story of Cortez or Pizzaro. Where the British decisively scored in the conflict was in their singleness of aim, direction and execution which was sadly lacking in the Maratha organization.

Since the establishment of Pax Britannica in

this country the Hindu has been brought into close contact with Western civilization; it is up to him to imbibe the purest and noblest that he can distil from it and,

> "Arise as in that elder time
> Warm, energetic, chaste, sublime."
>
> *Collins.*

The sweet memories and sturdy traditions of our heroes are a priceless national asset. Dare we sensibly allow our youth to grow up in ignorance of our splendid heritage and to fritter away life in aimless mimicry and devoid of the higher sense of duty towards the corporate existence of the nation? Hero-worship is the strongest article of faith of practically every great nation of the world. Great Britain not only reveres the memories of Drake, Nelson, the Duke of Wellington and her innumerable other heroes who won undying personal glory, but has in recent times perfected the very principle of national gratitude by raising a majestic memorial to the 'Unknown Warrior' who fought and died for the British Empire during the last Great War, "in that stately Minster whose most graceful office it is to enshrine England's immortal dead." And France followed suit. The military traditions of Germany are similarly personified in towering captains like Frederick the Great, Moltke and Hindenberg, whose achievements are held up as beacon lights to the youth of Germany. As Sedley has so aptly put it—

> "Example is a living law, whose sway
> Men more than all the written laws obey."

In fact chivalry, patriotism and heroism are as immortal as the currents which flow between manly hearts. The tremendous influence exercised by writers of fiction like Ballantyne, Henty and Rudyard Kipling in shaping the patriotic character and adventurous proclivities of British boys can never be over-estimated. We have an infinitely longer roll of illustrious names, that loom large in the history of human thought and endeavour than any of the modern nations of Europe, who owe their very birth to recent times as compared with the hoary antiquity of Hinduism. If tales were woven round these names, to harmonise with the spirit and gallant achievements of our heroes, what a magnificent pile of healthy and bracing literature could be built up to educate and inspire our youth, for the task of Tomorrow

It is of happy augury that Hindu leaders of the present age, princes and politicians, are all practically agreed on the vital importance of honouring the historic memories of our departed great, those stars of magnitude in the national firmament whose light has waxed brighter by time. The distinguished part played by the rulers of Alwar, Baroda, Benares, Bhavnagar, Bikaner, Gwalior, Indore, Jaipur, Jamnagar, Kapurthala, Kashmir, Kolhapur, Kotah, Marwar, Mewar, Mysore, Panna, Patiala, Rewa and Travancore to name a few of the States only, to crystallise and honour the warm sentiments of millions of our countrymen is too well known to students of Hindu politics to need any mention here. And at the crest of the continent, ensconced in the Himalayan fastnesses, rules the king of Nepal, the natural leader of the warlike Gurkha race, who has contributed equally lavishly to safeguard our national culture. There is again hardly a Hindu politician of note, from Rameshwaram in the South to Peshawar in the North and from Karachi in the West to Mandalay in the East, who has not assiduously helped to enrich the popular reverence for our ancient traditions, which reach far back into the dim confines of the world's youth.

*　　*　　*

After the third chapter of this book had come out of print, I happened to visit Jaipur, where I learnt from authoritative quarters that there is not a trace in the State historical records to bear out the allegation of Rajput princesses having ever been given in marraige to some of the Mogal emperors. My own remarks on this subject are based on the statements of Colonel Tod. But I quite agree with the Thakur Sahib of Jobner that Colonel Tod's Annals and Antiquities of Rajasthan are neither the last word in accuracy nor exhaustive and that the history of Rajasthan, if re-written after careful researches, would be considerably different. It is certainly not the first time that the theory of these matrimonial alliances has been disputed and denied by un-biassed scholars of repute. Although I do not propose to enter into an elaborate discussion of the subject here, yet I cannot refrain from making a few passing observations. One has certainly to tax the imagination to an extraordinary degree to believe that any of the Rajput rulers, invariably chivalrous, conservative and highly sensitive in matters of female honour, could have stooped so low as to marry a real Rajput princess to any Mogal emperor. Again it appears inconceivable that Rajput ladies of rank could possibly have consented to such degrading proposals in view of the fact that even the average Rajput female always preferred death to dishonour, of which history furnishes countless instances. This welter of doubt and disbelief is heavily augmented by the fact that not only Rajput but the whole of Hindu society was far far more conservative in its practical outlook on life during Mogal times than it now is. And to ask the meekest Hindu even today to give away his daughter in marraige to a Non-Hindu is an unforgivable insult, which marks the depth of the national sentiment. How then can one easily ignore the rigid morals and manners of Rajasthan of three hundred years ago and the compact mass of public opinion which enforced their universal observance ?

* * *

To collect the materials for this book, I have drawn from multifarious sources. As it has been purely designed, however, for popular reading, rather than as a dogmatic dissertation on History, I will not inflict a bibliography on the reader which necessarily lends an air of technicality to a work of this kind. The furious swirl of life leaves little leisure to the mass mind to delve into hair splitting questions of historical technique and deliberate on them.

* * *

I owe an apology to the reader for being unable to provide the picture of Suraj Mal of which I could not secure any copy till now, inspite of persistent efforts in various directions.

I must express my obligations to my friend Mr. Rishabh Charan Jain, who has already won his laurels as an author in the domain of Hindi literature, for various helpful suggestions and uniform courtesy which I have received from him in the publication of this book.

I am very grateful to Lt. Colonel H. L. O. Garrett, who has kindly written the Foreword at my request. That my modest effort should be appreciated by such an eminent scholar of history is in itself a matter of no small gratification and encouragement to me.

Hem Chandra Rai, M. A.

Delhi-Shahdara,
January, 1932.

# Chapter 1.

# Memories of Mewar.

"Clime of the unforgotten brave
Whose land from plain to mountain cave
Was freedom's home or glory's grave".

*Byron.*

An air of sanctity pervades the very name of Mewar. Although little bigger than Holland, it has, for centuries in the past, produced countless heroes and heroines in every stage of society who have set the highest standards in human valour, chastity, patriotism, self-sacrifice and in short the whole gamut of human virtue. Mewar has had to maintain a constant armed struggle for existence among powerful foes. Wedged in between the Pathan kingdoms of Delhi, Malwa and Gujerat, it held its own against the Pathans until the latter were overpowered by the Mogals in 1526. Thereafter Mewär had to contend single-handed against the concentrated power of the Mogal emperors, aided as they were by the Rajput rulers of other states in Rajasthan.

That the rulers of Mewar were able to safeguard their independence and national civilization through age after age of storm and stress, is due to the magnificent sacrifices of every clan among the Rajputs from time to time, commensurate with the gravity of the perils that arose. As a matter of fact the sons and daughters of Mewar have shed their blood so lavishly at the pure altar of duty that it is difficult to find a parallel in the domains of history, ancient or modern. With the Rajput every sacrifice made in the cause of the country or national honour was a matter of duty, intelligently understood and spontaneously carried out.

Sparta occupied a similar position to Mewar in the hegemony of ancient Greece and the Spartans certainly rose equal to the Rajputs in physical valour. Here the comparison, however, abruptly ends. The Spartan warrior was the finished product of the famous military discipline founded by Lycurgus. Every boy was taken away from his home at the age of 7 by the State and put through the public training house for 13 long years. Imagine the nature of the training imparted to the Spartan boy. Apart from gymnastics and military exercises the boy was made to suffer by hunger, thirst, exposure, floggings and torture in order to mould him into an efficient soldier, fearless, seized the Spartan boy, body and soul, from his early boyhood and kept him in a relentless military bondage as long as he was fit to bear arms

How could such a system appeal to a nation richly endowed with mental culture and a very high scale of civilization? The Rajput, an ornament of the Hindu race, with its refined and ancient civilization, took to arms from his earliest boyhood as naturally as the tiger takes to hunting. Compulsory military training was never known among the Rajputs nor was its need ever felt. Every Rajput was a born soldier and a conspicuously efficient one. Patriotism, honesty, chivalry, bravery and truthfulness were ingrained in his blood by heredity and tradition. The conduct of the average Rajput was based on sublime faith in duty. The great Rajput leaders of antiquity never found any dearth of fighting men among the Rajputs or any cause for dissatisfaction with their fighting qualities. There was therefore no necessity to dragoon the people as Lycurgus had to do to preserve the independence of Sparta.

The Spartan boy was not reckoned as a full fledged soldier until he had attained the age of 20 years. Such was not the case among the Rajputs. It is a matter of common history that Rajput boys well within their teens took part in regular battles and displayed wonderful proficiency in the use of arms. The Spartan girls again were put through a similar training as the boys except that they were not taken from their mothers. Physical beauty was no doubt evolved by means of this rigid system but it simultaneously robbed the Spartan girls of all modesty and womanly feelings. How low the Spartan girls stand against their Rajput sisters in respect of the ideal feminine virtues of the latter can be easily realised by even the most casual student of Rajput history.

In short the Spartan warrior was a mechanized creature made to serve a single purpose, viz. war, and bears no comparison with the Rajput cavalier with his lofty idealism, the priceless gift of ages of heroic tradition. The average Rajput is naturally gifted with a distinct personality in war, the importance of which quality has been so well developed by Von Bernhardi in recent times. The history of Mewar is rich with the heroic achievements of individuals, high and low, who acted on their own initiative when the hour of trial arrived.

As Frederick the Great observed "War opens the most fruitful field to all virtues, for at every moment constancy, pity, magnanimity, heroism and mercy shine forth in it". Mewar had to battle for its liberties against the successive waves of Mahomedan invasion for close upon one thousand years. That peace was never purchased at the cost of national independence constitutes the immortal glory of Mewar. Full many a time the devoted country stand on the brink of political annihilation but neither the rulers nor the people of Mewar could ever be persuaded to sacrifice the lofty principles for which they fought and died from generation to generation. If Mewar could have stooped to pander to the lust of the Pathan and Mogal emperors it could have saved itself from numerous murderous wars, with all the colossal wastage of blood and treasure in consequence. Had Mewar acquiesced even in a position of political vassalage under the Great Mogals it could have added enormously to its material resources and power. But then where would the soul of Mewar have been ? Surely not in the brightest firmament of human glory. "A just war is in the long run far better for a nation's soul than the most prosperous peace obtained by an acquiescence in wrong or injustice"-President Roosevelt.

* * * *

Let the reader now catch a glimpse of just a few, out of the innumerable heroes of Mewar,

> "Whose flag has braved a thousand years,
> The battle and the breeze."
>
> *Campbell.*

Roll back the mists of antiquity, and behold Bapa Rawal the illustrious founder of the present ruling dynasty of Mewar. Chittor was invaded by the Mahomedans for the first time in 713 A.D. under Mahomed Bin Kasim. But the invaders were hurled back with great slaughter by the martial prowess of Bapa Rawal, who next attacked Ghazni, subdued its governor Saleem and married his daughter. On his return to Mewar after this victorious campaign, Bapa Rawal was unanimously elected king by the nobles of the realm in 728 A. D. A few years later he took the field again and went conquering as far as Persia, Turan, Khurasan and Kashmir. He married numerous wives in various lands and left a progeny of 228 sons.

His descendent Khoman came to the throne of Chittor in 812 A. D. He had to face the second Mahomedan invasion under Khalifa Mamun, the governor of Khurasan and Sindh and a son of the celebrated Haroun-ul-Rashid. The rulers of practically every Rajput state of note in Northern India right up to the Parihars of Kashmir sent their contingents to the Gehlotes to help them in repelling this invasion. Khoman defeated the Moslems in 24 great battles and drove them out of Mewar. The commander of the Moslem host was captured alive and brought as a prisoner to Chittor.

By the time, however, that Samar Singh came to rule over Mewar the process of political disintegeration of the Rajput power in Northern India had gone very far indeed. The country was parcelled out into hundreds of small states. Almost every important town had its independent Raja, jealous of his neighbour and ready to oust him by fair means or foul. These petty princelings, belonging to different Rajput clans with their age-old feuds seldom acknowledged any sovereign. No wonder that Mahmud of Ghazni had an easy walk-over in his repeated invasions. There was hardly any serious fighting worth the name. Mahmud stormed the country, sacked numerous towns, destroyed their temples and returned to Ghazni with fabulous riches and thousands of slaves. Prithwi Raj Chohan, the so-called Hindu emperor of Delhi, partially succeeded in gathering the scattered Hindu forces under his banners. His sister, the beautiful Pratha, was married to Rawal Samar Singh of Mewar.

In 1191 A.D. the Afghans invaded India again under Shahabuddin Ghori. To meet the crisis Samar Singh was duly summoned from Chittor. He was put in supreme command of the Rajput army and while Prithwi Raj himself proceeded southwards to chastise the Raja of Pattan, Samar Singh inflicted a crushing defeat on the Ghori king and took him prisoner. According to the celebrated version of Chandra Bardai, popularly known as Chand, the bard and friend of Prithwi Raj, Mahomed Ghori with a blade of straw sticking from his mouth begged the emperor to treat him as one of his kine. On Samar Singh's merciful intercession then Ghori's life was spared by Prithwi Raj. Next year the latter carried away the beautiful Sanjogta, daughter of Jai Chand of Kannauj. A desperate running battle ensued, in which although the Chohan was able to get away with his bride, yet large numbers of his choicest warriors lost their lives in covering the retreat. While Jai Chand ground his teeth in impotent rage and invited the Afghans to attack Delhi again, Prithwi Raj was wasting precious time in the constant company of his lovely bride. The defence of the country was so grievously neglected that Mahomed Ghori came thundering up to the gates of Delhi, almost, without meeting the slightest opposition. Rawal Samar Singh was sent for at the eleventh hour. As he had already given up the cares of State and dedicated himself to a religious life, his consort, Pratha, advised him to disregard the summons from Delhi. But the aged hero reminded her that the invasion was not to be treated as a personal affair; the Hindu supremacy in Northern India was in jeopardy. So he arms and hastily mobilises his forces to strike the last blow in defence of the last Hindu empire of Delhi. On reaching Delhi he is shocked to learn that not the least resistance had so far been offered to the invaders. Verily the fate of Delhi was sealed. But the Rawal knew his stern duty and on the fatal banks of the Ghaggar, near Kurukshetra, laid down his life valiantly fighting the Afghan host in 1193 A. D.

* * * *

One full century has elapsed. The fame of the matchless beauty of queen Padmini inflames the lust of Alauddin, the Khilji emperor of Delhi. But as the Rajputs are lashed into fury by his base desire he determines to gain his object by force of arms. Chittor is besieged by the armies of Delhi; the siege lingers into weary months. At last Bhim Singh the noble spouse of Padmini is treacherously taken prisoner by the Khilji king. But the Afghans are soon outwitted by the Rajputs. While Bhim Singh is rescued, the Mahomedan army is held at bay by a small Rajput force under the gallant Gora and his nephew Badal, a boy aged 12 years. After performing prodigies of valour, Gora falls in the battle to rise no more. When the stalwart Badal, bleeding from numerous wounds, reaches Chittor all alone his aunt at once realises that her lord has died. Not a tear wells up in the eyes of the brave

Rajputni. She smilingly asks Badal to quickly tell her how her dear lord had fought as she does not want to tarry before joining him. The boy warrior briefly describes how magnificently the departed one had fought, brought down large numbers of the enemy including several chiefs to use them as his bed and gone to eternal sleep with a headless Afghan prince for his pillow. The Rajputni is glad beyond measure and soon jumps onto the flaming pyre to join her lord in *Amarlok*.

Meanwhile the siege continues and in 1290 A. D. is pressed with such deadly determination, that the devoted garrison, heavily thinned by continual battle, realise the approach of the final storm. The Maharana and his twelve sons are all within the beleaguered fort. Are they doomed to destruction ? The Maharana can save them all if he likes. But how can that high-souled ruler of Mewar even dream of such craven selfish conduct ? He resolves to save only one son, Ajey Singh, to save the dynasty from total extinction; all the other sons must be offered as sacrifice at the altar of Mewar's independence. So from day to day one prince is sent out by his royal parents to battle unto death, until the sublime sacrifice is over.

The great Saka is near at hand. Padmini in the full bloom of youth, beauty and love embraces

Padmini leading the *Sati* procession

her lord for the last time and then jumps on the flaming pyres along with the other females of Chittor, each more anxious than the other to preserve her chastity.

De Quincey has observed only too truly that "There is no man, who in his heart would not reverence a woman that chose to die rather than to be dishonoured."

The males clad in saffron attire rush out on the foe and die fighting sword in hand.

> "And how can man die better
> Than facing fearful odds,
> For the ashes of his fathers,
> And the temples of his Gods."
>
> *Macaulay.*

Within the walls of Chittor, the smouldering fires and heaps of ashes soon tell Alauddin how vain his quest for Padmini has been.

* * * *

Mewar had peace for over a hundred years. At the beginning of the 15th century the power of the Khilji emperers had decayed to such an extent that the governors of distant provinces like Golconda, Malwa and Gujerat had started on independent careers. In 1440 A. D. the combined armies of Malwa and Gujerat under the personal command of their respective kings Mahmud Shah and Ahmad Shah, invaded Mewar in great strength. Luckily Mewar was then under the sway of Maharana Kumbho, one of the greatest of its rulerrs. A great battle was fought at the border of the three kingdoms. The Maharana skilfully directed the operations in person and inflicted a crushing defeat on the allied Mahomedan armies. Mahmud Khilji, the king of Malwa, was taken prisoner along with thousands of the Mahomedan rank and file, while Ahmad Shah sought his safety in flight. The victorious Rajputs carried Mahmud to Chittor where he passed six months in honourable captivity, after which period he was magnanimously set free by the Maharana. The splendid Tower of Victory, Kirtistambh, at Chittor was built in honour of this victory.

Mewar reached the pinnacle of her glory during the reign of Maharana Sangram Singh from 1509 to 1530. His life is a record of continual war against the Mahomedan kings of Delhi and Malwa, who felt alarmed by the growing power of Mewar and took the offensive against her practically year after year. But the intrepid Maharana, to whom all the other chiefs of Rajputana and Central India owed allegiance, invariably defeated his Mahomedan foes often with enormous slaughter. After capturing Delhi in 1526, Babar realised the danger which the compact power of Mewar spelled for him. Accordingly he resolved to try conclusions with the Maharana and marched his army close to Bayana. The Mogal vanguard was however cut to pieces by the Rajputs. But the indomitable Babar, who had never lost heart in adversity, succeeded in winning over Shiladitya, a Tanwar Rajput chief, who enjoyed the confidence of the Maharana. Attempts at negotiation having failed, the two armies engaged in mortal strife. As soon as the traitor Shiladitya found his opportunity, he deserted the Rajput army along with 30 thousand troops of the vanguard under his command and went over to the enemy. Thus did the base perfidy of a national traitor canvass the defeat of his liege lord Maharana Sangram Singh. And the same battle furnishes an example of heroic self sacrifice. The only son of the ex-king, Ibrahim Lodi, who had come to the aid of the Maharana with an Afghan contingent, laid down his life on the battlefield.

At the time of his death the royal warrior of Mewar was verily a human wreck. The loss of an eye, an arm and a leg, as well as eighty odd scars of wounds on his body bore eloquent testimony to the numerous battles in which the Maharana had, at close quarters, fought the foes of his race and country.

* * * *

The nobles of Mewar having become disgusted with the misrule of Maharana Bikramaditya, a son of Maharana Sangram Singh, deposed him and raised his half-brother Ban Bir to the throne of Mewar. Udai Singh, the six year old son of the late Maharana, was also an inmate of the palace at Chittor. He was in charge of Panna, a brave nurse of the Khichi clan. Immediately after his accession, one night, Ban Bir made his way into Bikramaditya's apartment and slew him on the spot. As the cries of lamentation broke the ominous stillness of the night, a presentiment of approaching danger assailed the mind of the ever-watchful Panna near whom the infant prince lay sleeping peacefully in his cot. She became restless and anxious to learn the news when the palace barber rushed in and informed her of the foul murder that had just taken place. Instinctively Panna realised that Ban Bir would now be coming round to extinguish the tiny spark of Udai Singh's life. The murderer was at hand and she must save her future sovereign at whatever cost. She accordingly placed the sleeping prince in an empty basket, covered it with leaves and directed the faithful barber to carry it out of the palace as quick as possible. Forthwith the heroic woman placed her own sleeping son, who was about the prince's age, in the royal cot and began to await developments. Not long had she to wait. Holding a reeking sword in his hand, Ban Bir presently entered the room and enquired the whereabouts of prince Udai Singh. Although the heart of the heroic Panna was breaking under the strain of fierce maternal emotions, she never allowed even a tell-tale tear to escape her eyes. She stood there as firm as her native rocks and pointed her finger towards the royal cot. The murderer needed no second indication and plunged his bloody sword in the bosom of Panna's innocent child. Bearing the burden of her silent and stupendous grief Panna hastened out of the palace after the dark deed was over and set out in search of the barber. She found him on a bank of the Banas stream towards the west of Chittor. She tried to place the infant prince under the secret protection of one Rajput chief after the other but each declined the grave responsibility for fear of the terrible consequences of Ban Bir's wrath. Eventually the stout hearted dame succeeded in handing over the prince to Asa Shah, the Jain governor of Komulmeer, who pledged himself for the secret upbringing of the rightful owner of Mewar. Soon as Udai Singh came of age, the gallant Panna was not forgotten and she enjoyed the full fruits of royal gratitude which her descendents are enjoying to this day. That a young mother should so coolly and resolutely sacrifice the life of her first-born child,a male healthy one of about 6 years of age,at the altar of duty towards her king and country is an accomplishment of which any nation may well be proud.

* * * *

It appears that the prince whose life had been saved so miraculously did not turn out to be so gifted in the martial virtues and statesmanship as his ancestors who had preserved the honour of Mewar unsullied through centuries of armed conflict against the Moslem. In 1542 the nobles of Mewar deposed Ban Bir, who founded the famous Bhonsla dynasty of Nagpur. Udai Singh was raised to the throne of Mewar. The very same year marked the birth of a Mogal prince,viz. Akbar,in Amarkot who was destined to be one of the greatest emperors of India and an inveterate enemy of Mewar. Having been brought up in luxury and ease, Udai Singh developed a luxurious disposition and, worse still, one of his concubines came to exercise inordinate control over him. On the other hand his adversary Akbar was born and bred in the school of adversity which helped him to develope great soldierly and statesmanlike qualities, combined with an intimate knowledge of human nature. After he had forced Amber and Marwar to acknowledge his sovereignty, Akbar turned his attentions towards Mewar. The haughty Seesodiyas could not brook the very idea of surrender and prepared for war in defence of their ancient liberties and the honour of the Rajput race.

According to Rajput chronicles Chittor was twice invaded by Akbar. In the first invasion Maharana Udai Singh was taken prisoner by the Mogals, at which one of his numerous wives, named Vira, was so enraged that she led a counter attack in person. The fury of the onslaught was irresistible and the Mogals broke into headlong flight. The Maharana was rescued and he re-entered Chittor amidst great jubilations. He was so profuse in praise of the bravery of Vira before his Sardars that the latter took mortal offence. They soon had her put to death and this unhappy event ignited the fire of a dangerous discord in Chittor. Akbar soon launched a second invasion of Chittor in greater strength than before. Udai Singh was advised to abandon his capital for the distant fastnesses of the Aravellis. From ancient times however there has been such a halo of glory about Chittor that it has never lacked defenders in its hour of peril.

> "Where's the coward that would not dare
> To fight for such a land."
>
> *Scott.*

It is significant that simultaneously with the hereditary nobles of Mewar, many patriotic Rajput chiefs from far and near, representing every important clan among the Rajputs, boldly stood forth as the champions of Chittor. But the two heroes who attained immortal renown in the historic defence were Jaimal Rathore of Bednur and Futta Gehlote of Kailwa. The doomed walls of Chittor contained an incomparably smaller number of Rajput defenders than the beleaguering Mogal hosts.

As the chief of Saloombar, the commander of the devoted garrison, fell fighting at the *Suraj Dwar* (the gate of the Sun) his post was taken up by Futta, then only sixteen years of age. His warlike mother and newly married bride simultaneously armed themselves to take part in the battle in progress so that the youthful Futta may not possibly be deflected in the stern path of duty by any lurking desire for the charms of his bride. Inspired by the loftiest human ideals and impulses the Rajputs thus offered continuous sacrifices from day to day. Futta saw his mother and his bride both fall fighting gallantly in the thickest of the battle. After he had himself performed matchless feats in daring and swordsmanship, the youth at last lay low on the battle-field to rise no more. The command now devolved on Jaimal who directed the operations with consummate skill, utter disregard of danger and tireless energy. But all these noble virtues were of little avail against the limitless resources of Akber's empire. While standing by his men to repair a breach in the walls, one night, Jaimal was shot through the forehead. As the brave Rathore lay dying and all hopes of successful resistance having vanished, he issued his last orders for carrying out the awful rite of *jauhar*. That was the last chapter in the terrible drama of destruction. The females burned themselves alive in their thousands on flaming pyres not only to save their honour but also to leave no attraction for the men to live after them. The males then clothed themselves in saffron robes, embraced each other for the last time and poured out of the fort sword in hand. They rushed on the mass of the Mogal army like famished beasts of prey, each driven by the desire to kill as many as possible before he lay still in death. The unequal battle was soon over and the Mogal armies entered Chittor in 1568 to behold the mortal agonies of a deserted and dying city.

What finer tribute could be paid to the extraordinary heroism of Jaimal and Futta than that their foeman Akber had the magnanimity to extol their martial virtues and perpetuate their memory by erecting their statues, on elephant back, in the courtyard of the Agra fort. There is not a Charun or bard of note in the whole of Rajasthan who has not immortalized the gallant deeds of these two great patriots in inspiring verse.

* * * *

Rich, thrilling, and sublime, are the memories of Mewar. Its forts and fields, halls and hills have been washed so often with the blood of martyrs, that the whole land is sacred from end to end. The venerable spirit of Rajput idealism still hovers over the land but it sadly looks askance at the average Rajput of the day.

# Chapter II

# Maharana Pratap Singh

> "For freedom's battle once begun,
> Bequeathed from bleeding sire to son,
> Though baffled oft, its ever won.".
>
> *Byron.*

Four years after the fall of Chittor, i.e. in 1572, Maharana Udai Singh died at the age of 42. Prior to his death he nominated his younger son Jagmal as his successor in violation of the recognised law of succession under which Pratap Singh, the eldest son, was the rightful successor. The chief of Jhalore, Pratap's maternal uncle, asked the Rao of Saloombar, the principal noble of the realm, why Partap's claim had been set aside. As the sagacious Rao was resolutely of the opinion that Pratap should ascend the throne of Mewar, Jagmal was called upon to vacate it in open Darbar in favour of his elder brother. The family sword was then girded on to Partap's side by the Rao in accordance with ancient custom and Pratap was unanimously acclaimed as the Maharana.

By this time the kingdom of Mewar had become greatly shrivelled in proportions owing to steady Mogal encroachments. Akbar had extended his empire by fresh conquest and had already succeeded in bending the other Rajput chiefs of Rajputana under the imperial yoke. In short the whole country, with the exception of Mewar, lay at his feet. No doubt the plains of Mewar were overrun by the Mogals, but the Maharana maintained his independence in the Aravelli mountains. The fact that Mewar had defied his authority rankled in Akbar's mind. He sent several cordial invitations to Maharana Pratap asking him to attend the court; but the latter knew the real purport of these overtures. His lofty soul could not brook the idea of vassalage to the Great Mogal, no matter how gilded and glorious a position might be assigned to him over the other Rajput chiefs who had already succumbed.

He was undoubtedly the noblest Rajput cavalier "sans peur et sans reproche" of Rajasthan. The Charuns who sang the martial exploits of his ancestors to Pratap found a ready echo of the purest sentiments in his fearless heart. Why should a descendent of the illustrious Bapa Rawal bow his head before any mortal man? Had not a long line of his warlike ancestors fought the Moslem hosts in past ages and held their own manfully against them? To

Pratap the exploits of the heroes of Mewar were a living force always impelling him in the direction of the noblest human endeavour. He determined to stake everything, his kingdom, pleasures, comforts and life itself, for the independence of his beloved country. It should be remembered that Chittor, the capital of Mewar, had already been taken by the Mogals and thousands of its soldiers had laid down their lives in the cause of national independence. Trade was at a standstill and agriculture in the plains country was practically extinct owing to the state of war which prevailed. Apart from the fact that the ranks of the able-bodied soldiers of Mewar had been sadly depleted by intensive war, the material resources of the Maharana had also reached a very low ebb indeed. Under these dangerously adverse circumstances the Lion of Mewar boldly spurned the soft allurements of the Imperial Court, with all the attendant safety and ease, with the utmost contempt. Pratap now made his preparations for war in a singularly effective way, in fact, the most effective which a small principality like Mewar could devise in order to meet the menace of invasion by admittedly the mightiest military power of the age. The whole plains country was laid waste far and wide so that not a blade of grass or an ear of corn was left for the foe. The inhabitants were ordered to forsake the plains and seek the shelter of the Aravellis. These orders were rigorously enforced under pain of death; that these were not mere threats was found by several unfortunate delinquents to their cost. Bereft of the slightest trace of vegetation or the presence of man, the whole country was turned into a howling wilderness.

Pratap fully realised the tremendous odds against him. His brother princes of Rajasthan had all submitted to Akbar with the consequence that they were now arrayed in arms against him; his own younger brother Shakti Singh had been driven by some early estrangements in the family to the court of Akbar. Pratap had neither money nor men to wage war against the Mogals and yet he swore that as long as he was unable to wrest back Mewar from his foes he would never indulge in luxuries or royal comforts. He had established himself in the fastnesses of the Aravellis along with his subjects. So intense was the zeal he inspired among his people that not one turned traitor inspite of all the blandishments of the Mogals. That gallant band of Rajputs with their infinitesimal resources but stout unconquerable hearts fought the countless hosts of the Mogal empire for over a quarter of a century until their prolonged and matchless sacrifices bore the desired fruit. The purest fires of patriotism and national self respect burned in the bosom of the

Maharana Pratap

heroic Maharana. He stood unmoved in the thick of the severest vicissitudes of fortune that can ever befall mortal man. And there was a grandeur in his simplicity which awed the hearts of his deadliest foes.

To prosecute the war, as best he could, Pratap had first to get hold of money. Surat was in those days the greatest emporium of trade between India and foreign countries and caravens laden with merchandise used to pass continually along the borders of Mewar. This was too near a prize to escape the eagle eyes of Pratap's veteran Sardars. They issued from their eyries in the Aravellis and pounced on the unwary caravens, whose valuables were stripped and carried off to the hills, until Pratap had secured a fair amount of treasure to meet his immediate requirements. These depredations struck such a widespread terror that Surat had to be closed as an emporium for a long day to come. Pratap lost no time in strengthening his hill forts of Komulmeer and Gogunda. The native Bhils who were already fired by Pratap's enthusiasm and heartily supported his cause were carefully trained and taught how to deal with the foe, should they dare to penetrate into the hills. Huge boulders of rock were collected at strategic points to command the passage of the hilly defiles. The Bhils were adepts in this kind of warfare and their native skill was strongly supplemented by Rajput leadership.

On his way back from the Deccan, after the conquest of Sholapur, Raja Man Sing proceeded to Udaipur to pay a visit to the Maharana. Accordingly a feast was made ready on the banks of the Udaisagar lake in honour of the celebrated guest and prince Amar Singh was deputed to attend on him. As the Maharana did not put in his appearance, Man Singh realised the deliberate insult and prepared to depart. Just then Pratap appeared on the scene and tried to pacify his incensed guest. It was in vain. After threatening to humble the Maharana's pride, Man Singh departed in a furious temper. Akbar was moved to the quick on learning this news. By insulting Man Singh, the leading Rajput vassal and the foremost military commander of the Mogal empire, the Maharana had given mortal offence to the emperor. Apart from the question of imperial prestige which had been so flagrantly flouted, Akbar was too shrewd a statesman not to see that if strong action was not promptly taken he would lose the allegiance of all his newly acquired Rajput friends. Accordingly an army of several lakhs was mobilised at Ajmer and ordered to invade Mewar under the command of Prince Salim and Raja Man Singh.

The Mogal army penetrated into the Aravellis towards the west of Udaipur and in July 1576 it came face to face with the Rajputs in the famous defile of Haldighat. Pratap had no more than 22 thousand devoted Rajputs under his command each ready to sacrifice his life for the independence of Mewar. The battle raged all day long and was undoubtedly one of the bloodiest ever fought on the soil of Rajasthan. Pratap who rode his famous steed named "Chetak" headed straight for the towering elephant of Prince Salim in the centre of the Mogal army. The charge was irresistible and the Mogals scattered before it like chaff before the wind. In trying to save Salim, his elephant driver fell pierced by the Maharana's lance. "Chetak" planted his forelegs on the body of the huge black beast which enabled Pratap to tackle Salim at close quarters. But the steel *howdah* saved the life of Akbar's first-born. The terrified elephant soon fled from the field extricating his royal master from his perilous predicament. A terrific slaughter however took place at the spot. The Mogals closed in to surround the Maharana while the Rajputs were equally determined to foil that purpose. Like a great lion at bay, the Maharana plied his ponderous double edged sword with deadly effect among the surging mass of his enemies.

"Where'er that mighty arm is seen
The bravest be, or late hath been."

*Byron.*

He received seven wounds from sword, lance and bullet but he grimly fought on as fiercely as ever. At last the battle reached a stage when Pratap's followers clearly perceived that unless the emblems of royalty were removed from his head, he would either be killed or taken prisoner by the Mogals. Accordingly the Jhala Sardar Man Singh, of Sadri, resolved to sacrifice his own life in order to save that of Pratap. He forced his way to where the latter was fighting and tried to persuade him to give up the fatal emblems. As Pratap would not agree the devoted Jhala chief snatched the emblems, put them on his own head and started off in a different direction, which drew the ferocity of the Mogal attack after him. By the time the heroic Jhala fell, the battle was over. Out of the Rajput force, 14000 men lay dead on the gory battlefield after they had sent a very much larger number of their enemies to the shades below.

Pratap rode away with a heavy heart to avenge his country's wrongs at a later date. A couple of Mogal Sardars recognised him and galloped after him in pursuit. Pratap and "Chetak" were both bleeding profusely from their numerous wounds;

yet the noble horse bore him bravely along. But the pursuit could not be expected to last very long as the Mogals and their horses were fresh and were rapidly gaining ground. Presently somebody hailed the Maharana from the enemy's direction and the voice sounded familiar. Pratap turned round in his saddle and beheld a solitary Rajput riding towards him instead of the two Mogals. It was his long lost brother Shakti Singh who, having witnessed Pratap's gallantry in the day's battle and his present danger, had rushed after the Mogals and cut them both down. The two Rajput brothers met in an affectionate embrace and Shakti Singh swore to stand by Pratap ever after. Before the conversation was over, "Chetak" sank to the ground and expired. Tears of manly sorrow started in the Maharana's eyes; he had never been so moved before even at the death of his dearest ones as he was moved at the death of his faithful charger. A memorial, a platform, was built at the spot where "Chetak" fell and stands to this day near Jharol, at a distance of about ten miles from Haldighat. Shakti Singh gave his own steed named "Onkar" to Pratap and saw him off towards the safety of the distant hills.

The rainy season had now commenced which forced the Mogals out of the flooded defiles of the shelterless hills. This provided a very welcome though brief respite to Pratap. As soon as the rains were over, the Mogals re-entered the hills and besieged Pratap in the fort of Komulmeer. While the siege was in progress somebody poisoned the well which furnished drinking water to the garrison; this calamity obliged the Maharana to leave the doomed place. But the Sonigurra chief fought in defence of the citadel until his last breath and so did the principal bard of Mewar who died fighting rather than ask for quarter. As the poet says—

> "One crowded hour of glorious life
> Is worth an age without a name."

The Mogals launched a general offensive after the fall of Komulmeer and captured the forts of Dhurmeti, Chapan and Gogunda in rapid succession. Udaipur itself was soon seized.

Pratap was now a fugitive in the mountains. Perpetual war had taken a fearful toll of his soldiers. However the very thought of surrender was as far off from Pratap's unconquerable soul as ever. Out of his secret haunts in the hills he would issue ever and anon to fall on unwary Mogal detachments to destroy them or to do as much damage as possible. One day Farid Khan, the commander of a Mogal force, swore by the Prophet that he would either kill or capture the Maharana alive. By the irony of fate the tables were however tuurned on Farid

Khan himself and he soon stood a captive before Pratap. The head of the insolent Mogal could have been cut but the chivalry of the exalted Rajput cavalier would not let him treat his fallen foe like that. The life of the Khan was spared and he was allowed to go back free after his arms were taken.

About this very time prince Amar Singh rounded up a Mogal party which was escorting the ladies of the Khan Khanan's *Harem* to the hill fort of Gogunda. The fair prisoners were brought before the Maharana who treated them very honourably and sent them back under safe escort to the Khan Khanan. Is it a wonder then that the Khan Khanan, the greatest nobleman of the Mogal empire, was so deeply impressed with the chivalrous magnanimity of the Maharana as to burst into profuse admiration of his noble virtues. Some of the Doric verses composed by the great nobleman in praise of Pratap, which are extant to this day, are gushing with the Oriental philosophy of life and the unreality of material possessions. All that is immortal is the glory of heroic achievement. Pratap had sacrificed everything to preserve the honour of his country, race and religion. He alone out of all the Rajas of Hind had not bowed his head before mortal man. In this noble strain did the Khan Khanan lay bare his generous manly heart. He sent a copy of his verses to the emperor who warmy appreciated the brave sentiments expressed therein. Akbar was fully aware of the sore straits to which the Maharana was reduced. There were numerous Mogal spies who roamed over the hills in search of Pratap and he had to do all he could to save himself and his family from falling into the hands of the Mogals.

One day Sital a bard of Mewar who happened to visit Delhi went to pay his respects to the emperor. The man took off his turban before he bowed his head to the latter. Akbar was greatly surprised and enquired the reason for this strange behaviour. Sital drew himself up with pride and explained that the turban had been bestowed on him as a gift by Maharana Pratap who had never bowed his head before any man. How could that turban then be lowered ? The bard had therefore taken it off before bending his head in obeisance. Akbar was visibly moved at this expression of a splendid sentiment and freely praised the Maharana before the assembled Darbar as the bravest of the Rajput race.

As the years rolled by, Pratap's position grew more and more precarious. The Mogals had multiplied their efforts to track him down. Luckily the native Bhils served him with conspicuous fidelity at this crisis and more than once saved his family from imminent capture. To preserve the children from the danger of wild beasts, the Bhils used to put them into great baskets which were hung up at night from tall trees. Perilous uncertainty dogged the footsteps of the royal patriot in every hiding place. At times sudden flight alone would save him from his pursuers. Wild fruits were taken to satisfy the pangs of hunger and sometimes they had to go without even these. And they braved thirst, thorns and unspeakable privations with equal fortitude.

On a crag of the Aravellis Pratap sits all alone, pensively gazing in the direction of the plains which stretch out in the far distance. Is he not destined to drive out the Mogals from his beloved Mewar and bring the sufferings of his people to an end? He falls into a reverie and dreams of the past glories of Chittor. The crimson banners of Mewar float over the blood-stained battlements of Chittor before the last Saka takes place. The blood courses more hotly in Pratap's veins as he witnesses the final phases of that colossal tragedy which is so ineffaceably seared into his soul. He starts to take a hand only to awake to the realities of his own sad plight.

At last a stage was reached when the terrible sufferings of his royal spouse and children began to break down the barriers of Pratap's steel determination. After all be was a human being and had endured far too much, all for the sake of abstract glory. It was the broken down health of his family and their agonised misery which finally wrought some change in Pratap's outlook. He began to reflect if it would not be wise for him to conclude an honourable peace with the emperor which the latter would be only too glad to offer him as had been so often suggested to him in the past. As soon as the Mogal spies learnt about the Maharana's reflections they informed Prince Salim who forthwith wrote to Akbar that Pratap desired to negotiate. The emperor was beyond himself with joy on receipt of this intelligence and great festivities were held at the capital. Prithi Raj, a younger brother of the Raja of Bikaner, who was a prisoner on parole at Delhi, was however extremely sorry to hear this news. The patriotic prince secretly admired Pratap, and was a gifted poet. He solemnly declared before Akbar that Pratap would not surrender even in exchange for the whole of the Mogal empire and that the news was obviously invented by some one jealous of Pratap's renown. As Akbar was sceptical about this view, Prithi Raj obtained his permission to verify the news by sending a private messenger to Pratap. The prince composed a magnificent poem in his native Bhaka in praise of Pratap, extolling his grandeur as a patriot and defender of Hindu honour, and despatched it to him with a trusty retainer. As desired by its author, the poem produced an electric effect on Pratap. The paltry clouds of doubt and misconception which had appeared on the horizon of his lofty resolves and gallant endeavour, were dispelled as if by a magic touch. He would never surrender: the very idea was a sacrilege.

All his resources having been utterly exhausted by now, Pratap realized that he could not reconquer Mewar. So with a sad heart he bade farewell to his dear native land and struck out westwards to carve out a new kingdom for himself on the other side of the Indus in order to preserve the honour of his race and religion. Merciful Providence had, however, willed otherwise. The news of the final departure of the Maharana was received by the people with universal grief. At this crisis Mewar produced a hero, Bhama Shah, the great Jain financier of Udaipur, who resolved upon a grand sacrifice in the cause of his country. He took horse and rode in search of the Maharana towards the Indus River. Their meeting was pathetic in the extreme. Bhama Shah laid all the keys of his vast hoards of wealth at the lotus feet of his royal master and implored him to effect the deliverance of Mewar. Pratap could not find the heart to refuse this spontaneous offering, presented in such a patriotic spirit and accompanied with an unspeakably earnest solicitude. It almost appeared as if the guardian goddess of Mewar had inspired the patriotic Jain to resolve upon his magnificent sacrifice.

Pratap's hour of vengeance for which he had longed so passionately had arrived. Soon as Bhama Shah had put him in possession of wealth, he enlisted a large force and silently started for Mewar. Little did the Mogals and their general Shah Baz Khan dream that the Maharana who was known to have migrated to far-off Indus would soon rush into their midst to hunt them out of the Aravellis. In the beginning of the year 1586 the storm broke on the Mogal cantonement at Dewar village which was surprised and the Mogals including Shah Baz Khan were cut to peices. The remnants fled towards the fortress of Amet. It was stormed and the entire Mogal garrison was put to the sword. Before the other Mogal forces could receive a warning Pratap rushed on the fort of Komulmeer and destroyed the garrison including their governor Abdulla Khan. Not one escaped alive. Pratap now rushed one fort after the other hunting the dazed Mogals out of the country until he had wrested from them all of his 32 forts with the exception of Chittor and Mandalgarh. By the end of 1586 the major part of Mewar had been cleared of the foe. Pratap raided the territory of Raja Man Singh. This resulted in a clash with the Kutchwahas who were repulsed and Malpura, a flourishing grain market, was plundered. All the booty seized from this town was distributed by the Maharana among his soldiery.

Akbar had his hands too full at this time to wage a fresh war against Mewar. The Afghans were up in arms in Bengal and the emperor was hard put to it to suppress their rebellion. Towards the North West the frontier was ablaze with the revolt of the Yusufzai tribes while the intrigues of Abdulla the Uzbuk in Badakhshan had stirred up endless trouble in Afghanistan. Accordingly Mewar enjoyed peace for the next ten years. Pratap conferred fresh *jagirs* on his loyal Sardars who had served him with such signal devotion and valour in the war against the Mogals. The terrible hardships which he had suffered during the protracted war had however left their adverse effects on Pratap's powerful constitution. In the latter part of 1596 his health began to decline very rapidly. As a matter of fact the hero was at the end of his mortal career and soon lay on his death-bed surrounded by his sorrowing veterans who had shed their blood with him on many a hard fought battlefield in the past. Something seemed to be weighing heavily on Pratap's soul. The Rao of Saloombar gently enquired the cause of this prolonged mental agony. At this Pratap expressed the apprehension that after he was no more, his successor prince Amar Singh as well as the nobles would take to the paths of pleasure and ease, which would lose them the independence of Mewar. His soul would depart in peace only if they swore to guard the honour of their race and country with their lives. All the assembled nobles and the prince solemnly swore to act up to Pratap's wishes. Their unanimous assurance seemed to satisfy his soul: his agonised features relaxed into a serene smile and he breathed his last in peace.

"With thee were the dreams of my earliest love;
Every thought of my reason was thine:
In my last humble prayer to the Spirit above
Thy name shall be mingled with mine."

*T. Moore.*

Thus passed away one of the greatest patriots of all climes and all ages. His annals are an epic poem in real life and he was the living embodiment of Rajput idealism-honour and chivalry, patriotism and martial excellence.

"Yes, ye are made immortal on the day
Ye cease the dusty grains of time to weigh."

*W. Morris.*

# Chapter III
# Man Singh

"Whose distant footsteps echo
Through the corridors of Time".

*Longfellow.*

RAJA BAHAR MAL of Amber was an enterprising and politic ruler. On the expulsion of Humayun from India, he allied his fortunes with Sher Shah Sur. Uniting his forces with those of the Afghan general, Haji Khan, Raja Bahar Mal participated in the attack on Narnaul, which was under the Mogal governor Majnun Khan Kashkal. The place was so closely invested that Majnun Khan was reduced to sore straits. The Raja now exercised his powerful influence to secure honourable terms for the besieged Mogal and his negotiations proved eminently successful. Full of deep gratitude for the old Raja, Majnun Khan Kashkal, on reaching the Mogal court, spoke to Akbar in eloquent terms of the courage, statesmanship and amiability of the Katchwaha chief. The young emperor was delighted with the moderation and honourable treatment accorded to his lieutenant. The noblest trait of Akbar's character was to appreciate merit and manhood. He lost no time in inviting Raja Bahar Mal to his court and attaching him to his own person. The Raja was charmed beyond measure with the affability of the emperor and sent for his son Bhagwan Dass and grandson Man Singh to attend on him. This was Akbar's very first essay in welding together the Hindu and Moslem which was the one great ambition of his life and in achieving which he succeeded so well. The vigorous alliance of the house of Amber was the greatest bulwark which the genius of Akbar erected for his empire against all foes, external or internal. Once that this new source of political power was tapped, Akbar found it increasingly advantageous to nurture the principle with a tender solicitude.

The immediate task which confronted the boy emperor on his accession to the throne of Delhi was to overawe the turbulent Mahomedan nobility. In 1560 Khan Zeman was despatched to subdue Baz Bahadur in Gujrat, but on reaching there the former was disposed to be rebellions himself. Baz Bahadur still remained independent until Abdulla Khan Uzbuk was deputed to Gujrat and subdued him. The Uzbuk proved even more refractory. He tried to set himself up as an independent ruler, which led Akbar to

Man Singh

march in person against him. His new Katchwaha allies proceeded with the royal army. Man Singh was yet a stripling. After some sharp fighting the rebels were defeated. Abdulla Khan made his escape northwards. Akbar had yet to overcome the revolt of the Mirzas who had made common cause with Mozaffar II of Gujerat. With forced marches the royal army relieved Khan Azam who was beleaguered in Ahmedabad. But the Mirzas were yet far from subdued. In 1572 Akbar decided to capture Surat, one of their principal strongholds. Throughout this troublesome campaign, the aid of his Rajput allies, headed by Raja Bhagwan Das and Kunwar Man Singh, proved to be invaluable. They were always at the post of danger, ready to sacrifice their own lives for the emperor. While besieging Surat, a party of 1000 rebels, including the leaders, broke cover from the fort and made off in an endeavour to join their main forces in Gujerat. Akbar with a small detachment of 15 men, dashed off in pursuit. They soon came up with the rebels and charged. In the action, which took place, Akbar, accompanied by Raja Bhagwan Das and Man Singh alone, was cut off from the others. His life was in imminent peril, and was only saved by the dauntless valour of the Katchwaha chiefs. The rebels were routed and soon after the country was annexed to the Mogal empire.

The same year Maharana Udai Singh died a fugitive in the jungles of Rajpipla, but his heroic son Pratap was fighting gloriously for the independence of Mewar. He was at the time strengthening the approaches to the Aravellis and awaiting the onset of the Mogal hosts. While returning from Kathiawar, Man Singh resolved to pay a visit to the gallant Pratap. A rich feast was laid on the banks of the Udaisagar lake for Man Singh but the royal host stayed away. The insult was too much to be borne by the sensitive Rajput. Man Singh got up and refused to touch the repast. Pratap soon appeared and upbraided Man Singh for having given his sister in marriage to the Toork. The latter exclaimed, "It was for the preservation of your honour that we sacrificed our own and gave our daughters and our sisters to the Toork". This unwilling confession brimming with an indescribable pathos, and torn at that unwelcome hour from Man Singh affords an excellent index to his noble heart. At least he never rejoiced in the matrimonial connections of his house with the Mogals. Raja Bahar Mal was the first of the Rajputs to marry his daughter to a Mogal emperor. After him Raja Bhagwan Das, Man Singh's uncle, married his daughter to Prince Salim. Man Singh can certainly not be held responsible for these events. He was too young and junior a member of the family to have had much voice in such weighty matters of policy. Man Singh deserves due meed of praise for his manliness and chivalry in acknowledging the social stigma which attached to his house on account of these marriages. It is utterly unfair to hold Man Singh responsible for acts committed by his ancestors. These marriages were clearly contracted under covert political compulsion and were hardly a source of pride or pleasure to any true Rajput, Kutchwaha or Rathore. The very first term which Ajit Singh of Marwar dictated to the Mogal emperor, as soon as he was in a position to do so in 1713 A. D., was the stoppage of "the compulsory marriage of their daughters with the king." Shortly afterwards Bakht Singh of Marwar and Siwai Jai Singh of Amber approached Maharana Jagat Singh II of Mewar with a request to purify them, to re-admit them to matrimonial connections with his house. The Maharana gladly agreed and the two chiefs swore not to give a princess of their house to the Mogal in future, effacing thereby the blot which had temporarily attached to their families. That these marriages were forced on the Rajput chiefs, could not have been proved in a more conclusive and honourable manner.

Man Singh was seriously offended by the attitude taken up by the stern Maharana and unfortunately the breach became irreparable. The incidents of the unpleasant meeting were related to Akbar, who could not but feel sorely apprehensive lest the terrible rebuke received by the young Kutchwaha prince might not serve to turn his and his clan's allegiance, which he had taken so much pains to secure. Accordingly Akbar decided to prosecute the war against Pratap with redoubled energy. All the resources of the Mogal empire were collected and concentrated for the subjugation of Mewar. While paying his annual visit to Ajmer in 1576, the emperor put Man Singh in one of the principal commands of the Mogal armies. The bloody battle of Haldighat was fought in the same year. Komulmeer had fallen and Dhurmeti soon fell. The Maharana was fighting against terrible odds for the liberties of his country. To him the loss of every single Rajput warrior was irreparable, hemmed in as he was on all sides, while the Mogal could maintain his legions at full strength by drafts from his vast empire. Therein lies the grandeur and sublimity of Pratap's patriotic struggle which won him the unstinted admiration of friends and foes. The generous emperor was himself touched but could not draw back for the sake of far-reaching imperial interests.

Can it be imagined that Man Singh found this unrighteous war a congenial occupation ? Far from it. It was a sheer unpleasant necessity imposed on him by his allegiance to the emperor. What satisfaction could be derived in shedding the blood of his heroic kinsmen in Rajasthan !

Akbar truly appreciated the sentiments of his Rajput allies and employed the first opportunity to call away Man Singh from the war against Mewar. The Usbuk nobility had sullenly looked at the favour shown by Akbar to his Rajput allies. The treatment and flight of Abdulla had incensed them even more than ever. Now that they found Akbar seriously engaged in a war in Rajputana, they considered it an opportune time to raise the standard of rebellion in Bengal. In order to better achieve their treasonable designs they sent repeated invitations to Mirza Hakim, the emperor's brother, to invade the Punjab, assuring him of the loyal support of the old servants and companions of Humayun. That young prince too had some old retainers of his father's time of whom the chief was Koka Shadman, a son of Sulaiman Beg Andjani. He prevailed upon the prince to consider this invitation a happy augury of success. Accordingly a small force was despatched in 1581 which crossed the Indus. But the attempt was half-hearted and proved abortive. The invading captain was killed at Peshawar and his force hurled back. Akbar was disgusted with the treachery and duplicity of the Mogal Amirs; some of his own court were involved in these proceedings. The only recourse was to rely on the fidelity and gallantry of his Rajput allies. Man Singh and his uncle were ordered to proceed north and fight the menace on the frontier. They immediately set out and, like experienced generals, halted at their Sialkot *jagir* for a few days to overhaul the equipment of their army before it resumed its march to the frontier. Raja Bhagwan Das also took care to strengthen the defences of the fort of Lahore.

When Mirza Hakim learnt that his first force was routed, he despatched another under Koka Shadman Khan, his half-brother. The Khan was a brave young officer and had won considerable renown in the Mirza's wars in Afghanistan. Man Singh had advanced up to Rawalpindi, while Shadman was laying siege to the fort of Attock.

Such was the rapidity aud secrecy of Man Singh's movements that Shadman was well nigh surprised under the walls of the fort of Attock. But the latter turned and a fierce battle ensued. The Rajputs who were burning with eagerness to have a brush with the Afghans, had their heart's fill of fighting. Victory shone on the banners of Man Singh, whose intrepidity and valour largely contributed to the success of the day. His younger brother Suraj Singh was no less conspicuous for his prowess, having slain Shadman, the hostile leader, in single combat.

Mirza Hakim now took the field in person. The emperor ordered Man Singh to fall back before the young invader. These orders appeared mysterious and inexplicable to the Kunwar. But Akbar the consummate diplomat, took a comprehensive and prudent view of the situation. If the two armies had met, the boy Mirza was sure to have been defeated by the veterans of the Imperial army. In such an eventuality it was more than probable that the Mirza would have fled to Turkestan and been welcomed by Abdullah Khan Uzbuk, who had since possessed himself of the country round Badakhshan. The combination and a possible invasion by their combined armies would have been ten times more formidable than the present. Accordingly Akbar wanted to entice the Mirza into the interior of the Punjab. Flushed with the recent victory, Man Singh fell back reluctantly, and shut himself up in Lahore, along with his uncle and Syed Hamid Barha. Mirza Hakim was naturally encouraged at what he considered the pussilanimity of the foe. He marched up to Lahore and encamped in the gardens of Mehdi Kasim Khan on the banks of the Ravi. Akbar had issued strict orders to his generals to content themselves with repelling the attacks of Mirza Hakim, who was under no circumstances to be assaulted. His attacks were easily repulsed by the besieged. Akbar had meanwhile begun a swift advance towards Lahore; he had learnt that the orthodox party within Lahore had commenced intriguing with the invader. His intention was clearly to envelope the Mirza on all sides and capture him. The latter was not aware of his danger, being under the impression that Akbar was busy fighting his treacherous Amirs in far away Bengal. Suddenly the Mirza learnt that Akbar, at the head of the Imperial army, was close at hand in Sirhind; and fled precipitately towards the Indus.

Akbar let loose the Rajputs again who under Kunwar Man Singh rushed after the fugitives but received orders to stop at Peshawar. Prince Murad was also sent up with a Mogal force to effect a junction with Man Singh. The whole army then marched to Kabul under the generalship of Man Singh. Akbar followed leisurely in person. The Mirza was terrified and sued for pardon. Some of the Mahomedan Amirs who had corresponded with him advised Akbar to accept the overtures and retire to the Punjab. Akbar was not to be fooled so easily. The guarantees which he demanded from the Mirza for future good conduct were not forthcoming and the advance was therefore continued. Man Singh and Murad were approaching the vicinity of Kabul when their rear was attacked by Faridoon, the maternal uncle of the Mirza. The Mogal treasure loaded on camels, which was under the command of Kulich Khan was plundered by the Afghans. By the time Man Singh had time to turn back to grapple with the daring foe, even the camels had been dragged into the dangerous defiles. The plunderers escaped safely with their rich booty.

Man Singh wanted the Mirza to come down the heights of Khurd Kabul and fight. Snow had no terrors for the intrepid Rajput prince, just budding into lusty manhood. He delighted in riding on the snow clad hills at all hours of the day. One night the Afghans burnt huge bonfires on the hills, beating their tomtoms, shouting and howling all the time. This was one of their favourite tricks to frighten and worry the Indian army, who expected a night attack and made elaborate preparations. The night passed away in a futile state of alarm. Early in the morning hours the Mirza emerged from a defile to lead the attack. A hot action took place. The skillful Kutchwaha general stood on an eminence, intently watching every phase of the fighting and giving clear directions. Within a couple of hours the fight was over. The Afghans ran back like rabbits to the warrens of their hills, with the Rajputs of the vanguard at their heels.

Next morning Faridoon appeared at the head of the Afghan host and heavier fighting took place than the day before. The Rajput contingent again bore the brunt of the fighting. Man Singh was keenly watching from his position of vantage with practised eye. Due to the hilly nature of the ground isolated groups were fighting here and there. The whole of the Rajput force was engaged. Fresh bodies of Afghans swarmed up and a sudden rush seemed to overwhelm the Rajputs who were fighting desperately with superior numbers. Man Singh realised the peril of the situation and ordered the royal elephants to charge. The huge black beasts rushed into the thick of the Afghan host with upturned trunks and terrific yells, which ricochetted over and over again in the bleak hills. The charge was irresistible. Hundreds of the Afghans were crushed to pulp and the remnants fled back helter skelter into the hills, closely pursued by the victorious Rajputs.

The Afghans suffered so severely in this encounter that all the fighting was knocked out of them. Man Singh conveyed the glad tidings of victory to Akbar who was exceedingly pleased with his clever conduct of the operations. On reaching Kabul the magnanimous Akbar pardoned Mirza Hakim and bestowed the country back on him. The victorious

Mogal army retraced its steps to India. Man Singh was appointed governor of Peshawar. This important political charge was administered by him with conspicuous ability. He maintained stern military discipline and put down the lawlessness of the frontier tribes by swift punishment. The implicit trust reposed by the emperor in the House of Amber is further strikingly illustrated by the fact that a couple of years after *i. e.*, in 1584, Raja Bhagwan Das was appointed governor of the Punjab, while the gateway of the Mogal empire was being simultaneously guarded by his nephew, Kunwar Man Singh.

Meanwhile excessive drinking was hurrying Mirza Hakim into a premature grave. Learning that the Mirza was on his deathbed in 1588, Akbar ordered Man Singh to hasten to Kabul. He reached Kabul after the Mirza had expired. Faridoon the firebrand was disposed to be hostile and intended to send over the Mirza's children to Abdulla Khan Uzbuk. However, Akbar sent assurances in time and this coupled with the frank suavity of the young Rajput commander inspired the Afghan chiefs with confidence. Faridoon as well as the other recalcitrant Sirdars poured in gradually to pay their respects to Man Singh whose firm but sympathetic rule in Kabul won over the hearts of the Afghans. His wise statesmanship succeeded in persuading their stiff-necked chiefs to take service under the emperor. Leaving his eldest son Juggut Singh to rule the country, Man Singh conducted the Mirza's children to India. They were graciously treated by the emperor who was then in Rawalpindi and conveyed to the Imperial Harem. Another important event of the year was the conquest of the fair land of Kashmir by Raja Bhagwan Das and its annexation to the Mogal empire.

During the same year (1587) a difficult commission awaited Man Singh. The fierce Yusufzai tribes were in revolt and had already destroyed a considerable Mogal army. Of its two generals Raja Bir Bal had lost his life and Zain Khan had fled. The situation had grown very serious owing to these reverses. Accordingly the emperor put Man Singh and Todar Mal in surpreme command of the Mogal army which was appointed to assail the Yusufzai country. The compaign was a trying one. Not only was the country ragged and uncertain, but the guerilla tactics of the warlike and elusive foe were highly disconcerting. In the face of these disadvantages the veteran generals of the Mogal army proceeded cautiously and steadily stamped out the resistance of the tribesmen. Man Singh and his colleague penetrated the heart of the Yusufzai country, teaching a sharp lesson as they progressed. Military posts were established all over and those who refused to acknowledge the authority of the emperor were either killed or driven from the country. The moral effect of these relentless measures was so salutary that Abdulla began to tremble for the safety of his own small kingdom of Badakshan. He sent ambassadors with valuable presents and quickly made his peace with Akbar.

While Man Singh was chasing the Yusufzais over the frontier hills, Raja Bhagwan Das had been sent over to govern Kabul. There he became insane. Man Singh therefore went back to relieve his uncle at Kabul. It was over an year since the Rajputs had ruled over Afghanistan. The country was fairly tame but in 1588 the Mullas began to send complaints to Akbar about Rajput high-handedness in religious matters. In order to appease the popular clamour Akbar transferred Man Singh to the government of Behar, where Hindu Zemindars and Afghans were raising rebellious heads.

Man Singh reached Patna in 1589. The very first thing he did was to subdue Raja Puran Mall, the Zemindar of Hajipur, who had been looting the neighbouring districts in defiance of the Imperial authority. He was forced to disgorge his rich spoils and give his daughter in marriage to the younger brother of Man Singh. Some Mogal rebels, who were holding out in the eastern parts, were effectively dealt with by Kunwar Juggut Singh, who reduced them to submission by capturing their food and war stores with a swift *coup de tat.* On the 10th November 1589, the old Raja Bhagwan Das passed away at Lahore. Akbar called Kunwar Man Singh to court and in January 1590 formally invested him with the *Rajagi* of the House of Amber. Several rich gifts and the rank of Panj Hazari were also bestowed on him simultaneously. Man Singh returned to Behar loaded with honours and every mark of Imperial favour. He put the fortress of Rohtas into proper repairs and built some fine stone buildings inside for his own residence.

Man Singh now resolved to wrest Orissa from the Afghans who were holding it in force. The death of Sulaiman Kerarani had left Orissa in the hands of Katlu, an able chief. Under the brave Kunwar Juggut Singh, the royal army penetrated the country in the middle of the rainy season. Every stream was flooded. The country was a vast swamp. The martial prince pressed the Afghans so hard that they sued for peace and pardon. This led to a trap in which the treacherous foe inveigled him. The negotiations were protracted so long that Afghan reinforcements found time to rush up and Juggut Singh was taken prisoner. Man Singh now moved in person to retrieve this unexpected disaster. Luckily Katlu Khan died a few days after and the Afghans were so harassed and dispirited that they released Juggut Singh and surrendered to Man Singh. One hundred and fifty elephants, with other rich gifts, taken from the Afghans, were despatched as presents to the emperor at Delhi.

Hardly a couple of years had elapsed when the Afghans were up in arms again. So long as Isa Khan, the guardian of Katlu's children was alive, the peace treaty was scrupulously observed by him. His death in 1592 provided another opportunity to the Afghans for revolt. Their encroachments overspread the holy land of Jagan Nath. Man Singh was only too pleased. He determined to crush their rebellious heads effectually this time. A large and well equipped force assailed the Afghans from several quarters, and inflicted a heavy defeat on them in a pitched battle. They were pursued with great slaughter by Man Singh right up to the walls of Cuttuk. The Afghans sought sanctuary with the Hindu chief of the town, which was besieged by the Mogal army but eventually capitulated. The whole country up to the shores of the Bay of Bengal was then formally annexed by Man Singh to the Mogal empire. Over a hundred elephants with other treasures were again sent, as spoils of war, to the emperor. Having effectually crushed all the foes of the empire, Man Singh, in response to an invitation from Akbar, proceeded to court leading in his train scores of subdued chiefs to pay their homage to him.

As a further mark of his appreciation and confidence, Akbar appointed Man Singh as governor of all the three provinces of Behar, Orissa and Bengal. On return from court, Man Singh selected Akmahal for his seat of government. A great fort was erected here to uphold the royal authority and prestige in these distant provinces. In 1595 the Raja of Cooch Behar presented himself at the court of the great governor and acknowledged the sovereignty of the Mogal.

Next year his brave and capable son Juggut Singh was entrusted by Akbar with the government of the hill tracts in the Punjab. His second son Himmat Singh died of cholera the same year. Yet another misfortune was in store for him. Isa Khan, an Afghan chief, broke out into rebellion a few months after. Man Singh deputed his son Durjan Singh to put down the rebel. The treachery of a Mogal officer, however, brought the young Rajput prince into an ambush. A fierce but hopeless fight took place and the prince fell fighting at the head of his men who all perished. Struck with remorse and repentence for his misdeeds the rebel Isa Khan soon after surrendered all the treasures he had looted and even his sister, before he was granted pardon. It came too late however to recall the precious life which had been lost.

The Mogal armies had been wasting their energies in the Deccan since several years in the vain attempt to conquer the Mahomedan kingdoms of Ahmadnagar, Bijapur and Golconda. In 1599 Akbar resolved to proceed in person to direct the operations in the Deccan and ordered Man Singh to join him with all the available troops from the eastern provinces. Peace reigned within the empire at this time. Abdulla was no more in Turkestan. Pratap had entered the abode of the immortals in 1597: his son Amar Singh was still bidding defiance in Mewar to the Imperial arms. The subjugation of Mewar was as far off as ever. His failure to achieve it was a bitter mortification to Akbar. He desired to make one more attempt to gain his cherished purpose. Man Singh was therefore directed to join all his forces with those of Prince Salim and invade Mewar. Kunwar Juggut Singh was promoted to fill the governorship of Bengal. While on his way to that province, the Kunwar suddenly died at Agra. The Kutchwaha race was plunged in universal mourning at this sad and irreparable loss. His son Mahan Singh was accordingly made to succeed. Finding a young man of 16 years of age at the head of the government in Bengal, the headstrong Afghans once more broke out into open revolt. Contrary to expectations they assembled in strength, defeated the royal army at Bhadrak, and overran a large part of the province. The projected invasion of Mewar was abandoned by the emperor on receipt of these distracting news. Man Sinh was once more requested to punish these incorrigible rebels. The old war veteran hurried to Bengal in 1601 and halted at Rohtasgarh, where a power-

rally was made. The Afghans had established themselves in force at Purnea, Bikrampur, Kahgarwal and other towns. A great battle was fought at Sherpur. The Afghans were decimated by the royal artillery. Their war elephants turned and fled crushing hundreds of Afghans in their mad career. The rout was completed by brilliant charges of Rajput cavalry. Man Singh moved swiftly after them from place to place delivering smashing blows in his old style. The Afghans were outmatched in generalship by their grim old Rajput adversary. At last they threw down their arms and surrendered unconditionally throughout Bengal.

Akbar was over-joyed by the magnificent victories gained by Man Singh, called him to court and bestowed the *mansab* of *Haft Hazari* on him. This was the highest dignity to which a subject of the Mogal empire could aspire and never before had this been conferred on any Hindu or Moslem. Till then, the Mogal Amirs had never risen above the *mansab* of *Panj Hazari*. The emperor Akbar passed away in 1605. Jehangir had the good sense to confirm the trusted old servants of his father in their appointments. While confirming Man Singh as governor of Bengal, Jehangir bestowed numerous rich gifts on him. These comprised the finest horse in the Imperial stud, which had been specially presented to his father by Shah Abbas of Persia. Referring to the gift of this horse, Jehangir mentions in his autobiography that "the old Raja would not have been more pleased if I had bestowed a kingdom on him." For one year the Raja ruled over the eastern provinces with eminent justice and moderation. Next year he was recalled to court by Jehangir, who was madly in love with the fair Nur Jehan, then the wife of Sher Afgan, and wanted to replace Man Singh by one of his unscrupulous kinsmen who would help to murder the gallant Afghan noble to secure the object of the emperor's passion. Man Singh was only too pleased to be relieved of the cares of state and obtained Jehangir's permission to retire to his paternal domains of Amber, where he enjoyed several years of peace and happiness in the midst of his family.

With the death of Chand Sultana and the fall of Ahmadnagar in 1600, the Mogal advantage had come to a standstill. Malik Ambar, the brave Abyssinian noble, had set up a prince of the royal blood as king, as he was fighting the Mogal for his king and country. The Imperial armies were feeling wearied and exhausted with the ceaseless fighting. In 1615 Jehangir requisitioned the services of the Katchwaha contingents. Man Singh responded to the Imperial summons by leading the Rajput contingents in person. Advance of age had not cooled his warlike blood. He was as eager for battle in his declining years as ever he had been in the impetuosity of youthful days. But this was fated to be his last campaign. He passed away to eternal rest in 1615, while battling in the Deccan.

> "Far may we search before we find
> A heart so manly and so kind."
>
> *Scott.*

Sixty Ranis became *sati* on his funeral pyre. Out of his numerous sons only Bhao Singh survived him and inherited the family estates, titles and treasures.

Man Singh was full and handsome in person: he possessed fair colour and large eyes full of fire. His brilliant military genius, aided by his rare talent for statesmanship, carved out a sure way for him to the highest rank at the Mogal court. Although he moved day and night in the midst of his Mahomedan colleagues and courtiers, he never allowed his religious scruples and obligations to grow lax. One day Akbar smilingly sounded him about his religious proclivities and enquired if he could count on the Raja as a disciple. Without a moment's hesitation the Rajput frankly replied that his life and his sword were at the emperor's disposal, but that he was a staunch Hindu by religion. The polite rebuke was enough for the sagacious emperor. Leaving his armies to besiege Cuttuck in 1592, Man Singh hastened to pay his devotions at the famous shrine of Jagan Nath. His truthfulness, refinement and steadfast loyalty multiplied the charm of his character. Akbar owed the conquest of several provinces and countries, the quelling of many formidable rebellions exclusively to the abilities of this great Rajput general and administrator. One of the prominent military virtues of Raja Man Singh was that he never unnecessarily hazarded his own person in a battle. Mere bravado would not induce him to place himself at the head of troops while attacking.

His mode of warfare was more scientific. He skilfully directed operations from the rear and always with marked success. As for his personal bravery it was unquestioned. With Akbar in Gujrat he slew at least six foemen, while the emperor's life was in jeopardy, having been enveloped by a flying column of the Mirza's. The Rajput allies of Akbar served a conspicuous purpose. They acted as a powerful counterpoise to the turbulence of his Mahomedan nobility. Every time the Afghans broke out into insurrection, he pitched the veteran commander Man Singh and his devoted Rajputs against them. It is hardly an exaggeration to say that the splendid services rendered by the brilliant soldier-statesmen of the house of Amber were mainly instrumental in the re-establishment of Mogal empire in India and its expansion, after the death of Humayun.

---

# Chapter IV

# Amar Singh Rathore.

"But search the land of living men,
Where will you find their like agen ?"

*Scott.*

In a great gathering of the nobles of Marwar in 1634 the destiny of Amar Singh, the eldest son of Raja Guj Singh, was being determined in an atmosphere of oppressive solemnity. The Raja as well as the assembled nobles considered the prince to be unfit to succeed to the *gaddee* owing to the 'dangerous turbulence' of his character. Accordingly the sentence of exclusion was passed on him and he was exiled from the land of Maroo.

It was a day of deep sorrow for Jodhpur. Clad in black robes, with black shield, sword and armour all of the same sombre hue, the valiant prince, in obedience of his father's mandate and the decision of his elders, quietly left his native land to seek his fortunes abroad. He went not alone. Hundreds of the companions of his youth and those who had shed their blood beside him on many a hard fought battlefield in the Deccan, his trusty retainers, voluntarily partook of their lord's exile. A mournful procession passed out of the town. Not one of these stern departing warriors was destined to return home alive. Many an eye was wet; many a manly throat felt choking. Out of the silent cortege, however, not one uttered a word of reproach nor cast a lingering look behind. Their hearts were too full of sadness for expression.

Amar Singh proceeded to the court of Shah Jahan, who was so pleased with the gallantry of the young Rathore as to bestow on him the fief of Nagore and a high rank at court. Soon afterwards when the emperor was contemplating the change of his capital from Delhi to Agra a quarrel cropped up between Amar Singh Rathore and the Raja of Bikaner over the question of the ownership of Chulna. As both of them were honoured grandees of the Mogal court Shah Jahan thought fit to interpose. Intrigue was rampant at the court where Amar Singh had several foes, of whom the bitterest was Salabat Khan, the brother-in-law of the emperor. The valour, physical strength and swordsmanship of the Rathore cavalier was so superior to that of any of his Mogal compeers, that although they were secretly consumed by jealousy and hatred of his prowess, they

Amar Singh Rathore

never openly dared to pick a quarrel with him. They were always on the watch for an opportunity to humble his noble-born pride and were not slow to avail themselves of the chance which now presented itself. Somehow they prevailed upon Shah Jahan to commission Salabat Khan for the investigation of the two rival claims to Chulna. Naturally enough Salabat Khan made out a strong case against Amar Singh and proved him to have been the aggressor. Shah Jahan fined Amar Singh and again commissioned the Khan to realise the fine, unaware of the fact that the latter nourished an inveterate malice against the Rathore.

Salabat Khan was overjoyed with the thought that he now held a trump card in his hand to humiliate his proud foe. Accordingly one day he demanded the fine from Amar Singh in open Darbar. This deliberate insult infuriated the latter and he forthwith exclaimed "A Rajput's only treasure is his keen sword with which I pay thee my fine here". Suiting his action to these words, the Rathore with a single sweep of his sharp *Sirohi* cleft the insolent Khan in two. A deathly silence overspread, the Darbar Hall. Shah Jahan being deeply stirred, rebuked Amar Singh. But the Rathore was boiling over with an awful rage and defied the emperor there and then. At this some of the Mogal courtiers, companions of the killed Khan, closed around the Rathore with drawn swords. The fight was bloody but brief. Amar Singh made short work of his assailants, every one of whom he slaughtered on the spot. The horrified emperor ordered the imperial guard to kill or capture him. Easier said than done. Single-handed the doughty young Rathore was faced once more by heavy odds. Surrounded on all sides by the soldiers of the guard, he fought like a lion at bay. His sword flashed with the rapidity of lightning and with every stroke hurried one of his foes into eternity. It was an immortal fight, one against so many. But he appeared to be invincible and was chopping off heads with fearful rapidity until the small remnant of his foes broke and fled. Amar Singh now rushed at the emperor to cut him down. But he fled for his life and shut himself up in the *zenana.*

Having thus disposed of his enemies, Amar Singh stalked back with calm steps. The Darbar Hall of the Red Fort in Agra presented a bloody spectacle. The marble floor was drenched with blood and was strewn with fragments of human bodies cut down by the mighty arm of the infuriated Rothore. The courtiers had either fled or stood shivering with a mortal dread in the far ends of the Hall and the collonades. Soldiers were also skulking at safe distances. Nobody dared to approach Amar Singh as he surveyed the scene of carnage with feelings of satisfaction. He had wreaked a terrible vengeance on his enemies.

The terror stricken courtiers and soldiers dared not stir as the Rathore coolly walked out of the Red Fort. Next day a heavy price was set upon his head by the humiliated emperor. Accordingly a *bira* was placed in a golden platter and offered to the brilliant court assembly. Anybody who picked up the *bira* would have to undertake to slay Amar Singh and to bring back his head to the emperor. The bravest of the Mogal nobility shrank from the fearful undertaking and hung down their heads. All the taunts which the emperor showered on their heads failed to produce a volunteer. At last Arjun Gaud, the brother-in-law of Amar Singh, stepped forth and broke the strain by picking up the *bira*. Everybody was amazed at the audacity of Arjun, most of all the emperor, who exclaimed "What ! Arjun, have you fully considered the dangerous nature of the task you undertake ? If not, I can still allow you to drop the *bira* before it is too late, although I much appreciate the loyal sentiment which prompted you to take it up." But Arjun knew better and replied "Your Majesty need have no misgivings. I have fully realised my grave responsibility and have resolved either to attain success in my enterprise or perish in the attempt." Arjun who had all along borne a secret malice against his brave kinsman, now repaired to the house of Amar Singh with a smile on his face, praised him for his peerless valour and advised him to make his peace with Shah Jahan. At this craven suggestion Amar Sing blazed forth with wrath over the ingratitude of the emperor. But Arjun ultimately succeeded in inspiring him with confidence. Together they set out for court. It was already arranged by the traitor Arjun that he would introduce Amar Singh into the royal presence through a low trap door in a palace room. On reaching the spot, Arjun asked his companion to pass in first. An entry through the trap door would have necessitated Amar Singh to bend his head. The very idea of bending his head galled the soul of the noble Rathore and he spurned it disdainfully. But the wicked Arjun quickly solved the difficulty by persuading Amar Singh to pass through the trap door by introducing his legs foremost. No sooner was his body half way through the wicket, then the traitor, who had been waiting for this opportunity, plunged his sword into the heart of the unsuspecting hero. With an expiring effort, Amar Singh slashed at the traitor Rajput and cut off his nose. But the hero was now no more.

Arjun hastily severed his head and carried it as a trophy to the emperor, feeling confident of having won his favour. But on learning all the details of the assassination, Shah Jahan was ill pleased with the despicable treachery of the noseless Arjun, ordered his face to be blackened, had him mounted on a donkey and paraded through the bazars of the capital. After this his head was struck off as a warning to other traitors.

The sad news of Amar Singh's decease was conveyed to his young consort, the brave Hari Rani of the noble House of Boondi. She resolved to become *sati*, the sublime sacrifice which only a Hindu wife can make for the sake of her love and constancy to her husband. But unless the corpse which was lying in the Red Fort could be brought to her the rite of *sati* could not be performed. Ram Singh, the nephew of Amar Singh, volunteered at this crisis to cut his way into the fort and bring back his uncle's corpse. This was a sheer impossibility. Ram Singh, although equal to the bravest of his clan in personal daring, was yet but a stripling in his teens and had just about a hundred followers. Any attempt on their part to snatch away the corpse from the Mogal capital would have been nothing short of madness. The small band would have been annihilated without the shadow of a doubt in leading that forlorn hope. The Hari Rani perceived all this too clearly and forbade her youthful protege from hazarding his life so rashly. Some other means must be devised. While racking her brains over the matter, in the midst of her overwhelming grief, a ray of hope suddenly flashed across her mind.

May she not appeal for succour to Bhalloo Singh, the younger brother of her spouse? The two brothers had fallen out in earlier days over a trifling point of honour and had separated. The mutual estrangement had continued unabated in the succeeding years. The Rani made up her mind and penned a touching epistle to Bhalloo Singh. "Maharaj," she wrote "your valiant brother has been treacherously slain at the court of the Toork, leaving me utterly helpless. I wish to proceed to *Swarglok* with my beloved lord by becoming *sati*. But his corpse is lying in the Red Fort under the orders of the Sultan. Your nephew, though as brave as the other males of your illustrious house, is yet a boy and therefore incapable of rescuing the corpse unaided. May I request you in my last earthly extremity to hurry to my help? If you do have a sense of honour, then I adjure you to hasten to taste of the joys of battle and to bring me my heroic husband's corpse. The hour of supreme test of Rajput valour has arrived." The letter was quickly conveyed to its destination by Kisna, the staunch family barber.

Bhalloo Singh's heart was torn by conflicting emotions on reading these lines. Chivalry and honour urged him to forsake the old feud at this juncture but the devil whispered in his ear to ignore the summons. Why should he go out of his way to court death at the call of his long-lost brother's widow? Accordingly he was inclined to reject the appeal of the afflicted lady. But his wife, a noble Rajputni, rose equal to the occassion and prevented him from forming such an ignoble resolution. She bravely accused him of being a poltroon and lashed him with her pitiless sarcasm. "My lord, you need not worry," she suavely suggested. "I know you do not relish cold steel. So you stay at home to look after the children and the household while I go abroad in martial attire to do battle with the Moslem". This tirade immediately produced the desired effect. Bhalloo Singh was stung to the quick with remorse and shame. He collected all his retainers and set out on the fatal expedition.

By forced marches they soon reached the castle of Amar Singh, near the Mogal capital. Their arrival brought joy to the drooping spirits of the Hari Rani and lit up with fresh hope the face of the brave lad Ram Singh. All told the Rajputs now made up a force of 600 sturdy men. With these desperate warriors, all fresh, well mounted and armed to the teeth, their leaders might reasonably dare to attempt anything. A short council of war was held. Bhalloo Singh decided to lead a body of 500 horse to the Red Fort to rescue the corpse and advised Ram Singh to stay behind with the other Rajputs to guard the erection of the funeral pyre. But the boy-warrior was not to be so easily denied the glory of participating in the approaching struggle in the fort. He strongly remonstrated with his uncle who had eventually to agree to satisfy the keen martial ardour of the young man. After all it was a question of precedence in the tragic drama of destruction which awaited them all. The spirited Brahmin priest of the family, then took it upon himself to guard the funeral pyre along with the Rajputs who were left behind.

The tasks having been thus assigned to the two parties, Bhalloo Singh delivered a short harangue to his men before starting for the fort. "O my brave Rajputs, we have to rescue the corpse of Amar Singh today for the sake of his noble wife. The soul of that great hero is watching our actions today. Have I to urge you to acquit yourselves honourably and manfully in the coming battle? You know we are marching into the jaws of death. But I see you are not appalled at this prospect. Is not the very sensation of fear a stranger to the true kshattriya? Uphold the traditions of Rajput valour worthily today. Sell your lives as dearly as possible. Death in battle is the happiest luck which can befall a Rajput. You go to people the mansions of the Sun. Remember that the honour of a noble Rajput lady in distress is in your hands. Swear to me by your sharp swords that you will follow me unflinchingly to the end."

Fierce passion was surging in the hearts of the assembled Rajputs; their eyes were flashing fire. They swore a mighty oath as their leader bade them. The troop of 500 desperate men then rode off to the fort at a gallop with Bhalloo Singh and Ram Singh at their head. The guards at the gate were surprised and put to the sword. Having thus forced an entrance, the Rajputs soon penetrated to the spot where the corpse lay exposed. They reverently lifted it on to the saddle of the elder leader, Bhalloo Singh, who seemed to be petrified with remorse and grief for the moment. But there was little time for emotion. He shook it off and ordered a rapid retreat.

By this time the alarm had been sounded and all the available Mogal army inside the fort had turned out to intercept the Rajputs and foil their purpose. Surrounded on all sides they had now to fight their way inch by inch to the gate. The bravest of the Mogals struck in in the vain endeavour to stem the progress of their foes who were steadily forging their way towards the gate. As their numbers diminished the Rajputs fought with an increasingly fiercer determination. They hacked and hewed with their double edged swords making a prodigious slaughter of the Mogals. At last a rousing cheer from Bhalloo Singh announced that he had safely passed out of the fort with his precious burden. Once outside he shouted an order to the Rajputs to resist the passage of the gate. The next instant he had wheeled round his noble steed and galloped off on the wings of haste to where the Hari Rani was waiting to ascend the funeral pyre.

With the remnants of the Rajput troop, Ram Singh held back at the gate of the fort to resist the egress of the royal army. The odds were overwhelming and it was only a question of time as to how soon the devoted Rajputs were wiped out. But they fought on valiantly actuated by one great purpose, viz. to delay the Mogals as long as possible. Every one of them tried to kill as many antagonists as he could before he fell to rise no more. The grim tragedy was soon over.

After disposing of the Rajputs at the gate, the

royal army came rushing up to the funeral pyre which had been just lighted, Before they could pollute the pyre they had to contend with the fresh Rajput warriors under Bhalloo Singh who eagerly awaited the onset. The Mogals were beside themselves with rage at being thus baulked of their prey by a mere handfull of men. The Rajputs stood bravely encircling the pyre like a living wall of steel and closed in deadly combat with their infuriated assailants. The flames shot up higher and higher from the pyre, over which sat the Rani with her husband's head in her lap. She was chanting a sacred hymn and seemed to be oblivious of the deafening din of battle all around her. The Rajputs were holding their ground manfully. Bhalloo Singh performed prodigies of valour and encouraged his men both by word and deed. He fell pierced by wounds at last. As his dimming gaze rested on the burning pyre, an indescribable sadness crept over his face. His soul was anguished by the thought lest all their sacrifices had been in vain. The Brahmin priest caught his looks, came up to him in the midst of whirling swords and whispered something in his ear. The face of the dying Rothore was immediately lit up with satisfaction before he lay still in death. The Brahmin too snatched a sword and joined in the melee. To the last man the Rajputs fought like heroes and fell like heroes.

> "Though few their numbers, their's the strife
> That neither spares nor speaks for life."
>
> *Byron.*

The pyre had practically burnt itself out by the time the Mogals had finished with their redoubtable adversaries and all that remained of Amar Singh and his consort was red hot embers and ashes. The thickening gloom of the evening shadows closed upon a fearful scene of death and desolation. Shah Jahan was extremely chagrined on learning of the failure of his numerous troops who had so thoroughly been baffled by an incomparably smaller number of Rajputs. The Bokhara Gate by which the rescuing party had entered the Red Fort was re-named Amar Singh's Gate and was ordered to be closed up in order to obliterate the shame of the Mogal army. This gate was opened in British times by the order of Captain George Steele of the Bengal Engineers in 1866. The memory of the heroic Amar Singh Rathore has been preserved in immortal verse by the Charuns of Rajasthan. And the depth of popular feeling can be gauged from the fact that bards have woven these stirring episodes into a rude play in Bhasha called the 'Saka of Amar Singh Rathore' which is staged in the countryside all over the length and breadth of Northern India.

# Chapter V.

# Jaswant Singh.

"Thee haughty tyrants ne'er shall tame;
All their attempts to bend thee down
Will but arouse thy generous flame,
And work their woe, and thy renown."

*James Thomson*

JASWANT SINGH ascended the *gaddee* of Marwar on the death of his father Raja Guj Singh in 1638 A. D. He was the younger brother of the famous Amar Singh Rathore. The young prince had already seen a good deal of active service in the incessant war which the Great Mogal was waging in the Deccan. In the wars of Gondwana, Ahmadnagar and Bijapur, he gave ample proofs of his gallantry. He was always to be seen in the thickest of the fight vigorously plying his *khanda* on the heads of the Deccani foe with the inimitable rapidity of the Rajput swordsman. His frame was tall and athletic. He scorned all danger in the field. The sensation of fear was an absolute stranger to him.

In addition to his personal daring in war he possessed clear brains and an unconquerable determination. Prince Aurangzeb, who commanded the Mogal armies in the Deccan, grew to respect and fear him. The latter feeling was intensified on his accession to the throne of Delhi and was abundantly manifested. Jaswant Singh was also a patron of literature at home. His various admirable qualities enabled him to fully maintain the honourable traditions of his noble house and the martial Rathore race.

Shah Jahan fell ill early in 1658; his sons started the scramble for empire in right earnest. Dara was at this time acting as Regent at Delhi. Murad was Viceroy of Gujrat. Aurangzeb was operating in the Deccan and Shujah in Bengal. Led by hostile aims the rival brothers made for the capital from their distant provinces. The cunning and craft of Aurangzeb easily prevailed upon the unsuspecting Murad to combine with him in fighting Dara and Shujah. The Rajputs, to a man, decided to fight for their rightful emperor, the aged Shah Jahan. Apart from this, the handsome, brave and frank Dara, who was fighting for his father, was loved more universally than any of his three younger brothers. The instant he got wind of Aurangzeb's warlike preparations he bestowed the *mansab* of *Panjhazari* on Jaswant Singh and appointed him

Viceroy of Malwa. This was probably done to make sure of his invaluable support, although there was little need of it since all the Rajputs were devoted to the cause of Shah Jahan out of a sheer sense of duty. Talboys Wheeler attributes Jaswant Singh's fidelity to the reason that he had married a daughter of Shah Jahan; but this statement is not verified by any other history. Jaswant Singh was deputed in March 1658 to check Aurangzeb who began his advance northwards at the head of the Deccan army. A powerful detachment of Mogal artillery under Kasim Khan was also placed under the command of the Rathore general since the Rajput contingents had no artillery. Dara was not for a moment deceived about the ultimate designs of the *Nimazee* as he called Aurangzeb. He knew that poor Murad was being made a catspaw by the wily *Nimazee* whose false cloak of religion preserved him from Murad's suspicions. He tried to warn Murad but in vain.

The royal army under Jaswant Singh took up its position on the banks of the Nerbudda about 14 miles from Ujjain. The combined armies of Aurangzeb and Murad prepared to cross the river and a fierce battle ensued on the 17th of April. The masterly intrigue of the former had already won over Kasim Khan and his Mogals. The traitor not only fired over the heads of the foe but soon ran short of ammunition which he had previously done away with. With the batteries lying idle, the passage of the Nerbudda could not be contested The two brothers easily crossed over under cover of heavy fire from their French and Portuguese gunners. Kasim Khan fell back at this juncture without striking a blow, dangerously exposing Jaswant Singh and the entire flank of the Rajput force. Without in the least being disheartened by the treachery of the Mogals, the Rajput cavalry charged boldly and came to handgrips with their foemen. It was an altogether unequal combat. Rajput valour was matched against overwhelming numbers and European artillery. The battle raged all day long without any side acknowledging defeat. The Mogal historian says that when a son of a Rajput fell the father smeared his forehead with the blood of the boy and rushed on the Mogals to avenge his death, which bears ample testimony to the terrific nature of the fighting. According to the Rajput chronicles ten thousand Moslems were slain on this day; while Aurangzeb in a letter to the king of Bijapur states, that six thousand Rajputs fell in the action. The Haras of Boondi and Kotah sealed their devotion to the emperor by death. Rao Ratan Singh, the Rathore chief of Rutlam, performed matchless

Vindumati *and* Jaswant Singh

prodigies of valour. Jaswant Singh and his faithful steed "Maboob" were dripping with gore from the numerous wounds received in the day's battle.

> "For Fame is there to say who bleeds,
> And Honour's eye on daring deeds."
>
> *Byron.*

At last night cast a pall of blackness over the battlefield and the exhausted combatants retired to rest. Jaswant Singh and his handful of Rajputs, who were left alive, made off during the night for Marwar. To wait till the morrow, would have been courting a futile and sure death.

The singular treatment meted out to Jaswant Singh by his queen, Vindu Mati, a princess of Mewar, illustrates but too well the magnificent Rajput ideal of loyalty to the sovereign. She ordered the gates of the castle to be shut to her fugitive lord and lamented his lack of spirit in not sacrificing his life in the cause of his sovereign. Her mood suddenly changed. She declared that her husband must have died fighting on the field of battle and ordered the erection of a funeral pile to become *sati*. However the earnest expostulations of her attendents soon prevailed upon her to desist from this attempt; but then she put on martial attire and rode out of the castle gate to go forth to battle in order to atone for what she imagined as the direliction of her husband's duty. It was with the utmost difficulty that the incensed queen was dissuaded and brought to believe that defeat was due to the sudden defection of the Mogals and that Jaswant Singh had simply returned to recoup his force, before he went forth to fight for the emperor again.

Aurangzeb moved fast after his victory on the Nerbudda. He had reached within 12 miles of Agra when Dara arrived to give battle. But this unfortunate prince was again tricked by an inexorable fate. Khalil Ullah Khan, the commander of a Mogal division in Dara's army, bore him a deadly grudge since his wife had been ravished by Shah Jahan. He was in communication with Aurangzeb and systematically thwarted Dara's good generalship until the two armies stood facing each other at Samugarh on the 7th June 1658. In the battle which followed, the traitor Khalil Ullah Khan withheld the aid of the 30 thousand Mogal troops under him, pretending to be holding them as a reserve. Even then Dara had well nigh won, having smashed his opponent's army. Murad was in a sore plight being hemmed in by the Rajputs while Aurangzeb was shouting at the top of his voice to rally his men in vain. Soon as the traitor saw that the day was almost lost to Aurangzeb, he prevailed upon Dara to alight from his elephant. This trivial action lost the empire of India to the unfortunate prince. The traitor made off. Dara realised his fatal mistake too late. Taking him to be dead, his army melted away and it was all he could do to escape with his life.

Aurangzeb met with few obstacles at Delhi. The ground had been excellently prepared by his timely intrigues. Poor confiding Murad was put in chains to be murdered in the fort of Gwalior. Shah Jahan was imprisoned in the fort of Agra. Aurangzeb was supreme. He had since also won over the allegiance of Raja Jai Singh of Amber who proved to be a veritable tower of strength to him in overcoming all the dangers and obstacles which were yet to be confronted. Jai Singh, who was a clever diplomat, actively corresponded with all the chiefs who had either fought against Aurangzeb or not yet acknowledged him as emperor. He brought round Jaswant Singh to agree to help in the operations against Shujah on grant of free pardon by Aurangzeb. Considering that he might secure a good opportunity for revenge, Jaswant Singh accepted this proposal and proceeded to join Aurangzeb's army which was advancing to meet Shujah. The two armies met at Kujwa early in January 1659. The moment the battle began, Jaswant wheeled round at the head of his Rajput cavalry and galloped to the rear of Aurangzeb's army. The Rajputs cut down the rearguard to pieces and plundered all the Imperial equipage and military stores. The enormous spoils were loaded on camels and the whole force marched on Agra in the hope of effecting a junction with Dara's army, who had been apprised of this project a week before and advised to rush up to Agra. The approach of Jaswant Singh put the partisans of Aurangzeb at Agra into mortal terror, whereas it raised glad hopes in the hearts of those who still remained faithful to Shah Jahan. Wild rumours were afloat inside the city. Bernier states that Aurangzeb's uncle Shaista Khan, the governor of Agra, was with extreme difficulty prevented by his women from taking poison out of fright.

There is a strong probability that if Jaswant Singh had entered Agra, Shah Jahan might have been liberated and reseated on his throne. Such a step was, however, attended with enormous risks. Jaswant Singh had learnt that Shujah was defeated and Aurangzeb was coming back in hot haste. In fact he was labouring under keen anxiety lest all his successes might be exploded by the unexpected manœuvres of the Rathore chief. Contrary to the latter's calculations, Dara failed to appear, since he was in the clutches of yet another traitor, viz. Shah Nawaz Khan, the father-in-law of Aurangzeb, who was assiduously entertaining the prince at Ahmadabad to delay his departure. Jaswant Singh was greatly disappointed at Dara's inactivity and considered it wiser under the circumstances to march back to Marwar with all the rich spoils secured by him in the plunder of the Imperial camp.

He bore an implacable hatred towards the crafty bigot, who had secured the throne by treachery and intrigue. These feelings were reciprocated even in a warmer degree by Aurangzeb, but he was politic and knew well how to bide his time. He realised that if Jaswant Singh with his twenty thousand devoted Rajputs went over to Dara, the consummation of his cherished desires might yet be as far off as ever. Accordingly Jai Singh was once more prompted to mediate. Jaswant Singh was offered unconditional pardon for his past behaviour, along with the viceroyalty of Gujrat, if he would only be neutral in the future. Dara had proved his incapacity and his cause had been definitely forsaken by the Mahomedan nobility. Jaswant Singh, therefore, accepted the emperor's offer and was ordered to proceed to the Deccan to join prince Moazzam in the war against Sivaji. What induced him to climb down to accept the proposal was to be soon revealed.

This is not a solitary instance of a Rajput of distinguished lineage who took service under the

Mogal against his natural inclinations. Scores were forced by circumstances to present themselves at the court of the Great Mogal. Of these the gallant Prithi Singh of Bikaner is an illustrious instance. Even the great general Man Singh seems to have been a prey of circumstances. There were others who were driven into the arms of the Mogal by the unkindly treatment of their own kinsmen in Rajasthan. They forsook their homes out of pique or despair. Amar Singh, Sakat Singh, Umed Singh, Sagarji are only a few of the historic names of noble Rajputs who were thus driven out and lost to the homeland. Indifference, harshness, injustice and insult cannot be endured by any self-respecting man, least of all by the sensitive, high-souled Rajput. Some had to bend perforce in those times of storm and stress. The warlike Chandra Sen of Jodhpur however never bowed his head before mortal man. Like the heroic Maharana Pratap he refused to acknowledge the sovereignty of Akbar and fought against his armies till his last breath. The Haras of Boondi exacted strictly honourable terms before acknowledging the sovereignty of the Mogal. That others were unable to secure all those terms, should cause no surprise or harsh comment. Uniformity in politics is impossible to attain owing to the changes of time, environment, expedience and numerous other causes. Let posterity try to understand in a spirit of sympathy and refrain from judging those who have gone by by hyper-critical standards.

On reaching the Deccan in 1663, Jaswant Singh *soon came across another opportunity for revenge* which he did not hesitate to seize. Sivaji solicited his aid in a plan of assassination of Shaista Khan, who was staying in Poona with all his force. The plot elaborated between the two chiefs succeeded so well that with the exception of the principal intended victim, who escaped by jumping through a window, his son and all his retainers were slain. The sparkling glamour of romance attached to this exploit went far to captivate the hearts of the Maratha people. On the other side, Aurangzeb ground his teeth with rage when he learnt of Jaswant Singh's share in it. He could not but dissimulate which he did with a good grace and went so far as to appoint the latter to the principal command of the Mogal armies in the Deccan. This was a stopgap arrangement, since Jai Singh the Mirza Rajah was soon sent down to take over charge from the dangerous Rathore chief. On the escape of Sivaji from Delhi, a few months after, the Mirza Rajah was suspected of complicity, which caused him to fall into disgrace. In accordance with his policy of arousing the mutual jealousies of the Rajahs serving under him, Aurangzeb raised Jaswant Singh to favour again.

About this time Aurangzeb fell seriously ill. The court physicians gave up all hope of recovery. It was even rumoured that he died. His sons began to intrigue for the succession. Jaswant Singh, Mahabat Khan and some other nobles took up the cause of Moazzam while another party favoured the claims of Akbar. Before it came to actual conflict the emperor recovered and became wroth with Jaswant Singh for having instigated Moazzam with designs on the throne. He always had something or the other up his sleeve to worry and tax the anxiety of the Mogal court.

> "A frame of adamant, a soul of fire,
> No dangers fright him, and no labours tire."
>
> *Samuel Johnson.*

Deler Khan was consequently despatched from Delhi to take over the command of the army from Jaswant Singh, who received the orders of his supersession with remarkable sang froid. The new general arrived at Aurangabab and was preparing to go to sleep when news arrived that the Rathore and Moazzam were rushing up to slaughter him. Rudely shocked at the incomprehensible audacity of Jaswant Singh, his would-be successor ran his hardest that night for the sake of dear life. The emperor was none the less confounded. Eventually he decided to offer the viceroyalty of Gujrat to Jaswant Singh. It was necessary to separate him from the youthful Moazzam so that the two should not hatch further mischief and play such dangerous pranks. Jaswant Singh reached Ahmadabad only to learn that he had been outwitted: another had forestalled him as viceroy. He had been long away from home and therefore in 1670 A. D. returned to Marwar.

By this time Aurangzeb had twice attempted to get him murdered, once while serving in the Deccan and a second time while passing through Gujrat. Both the attempts had proved abortive owing to the watchfulness and fidelity of Jaswant's retainers. The emperor was in constant fear of this powerful Rajah. Each wanted to revenge himself on the other at the earliest opportunity. 1678 the Afghans and Usbuks again rebelled at the northern outposts of the Mogal empire. Aurangzeb very politely invited Jaswant Singh to proceed to Kabul as his viceroy to quell the rebellion, knowing full well that the turbulent Rajputs would find more than plenty of occupation in fighting the fierce highlanders amidst the uncongenial snows. Naturally enough the emperor deliberated that in case the bait was swallowed by the proud chief, his destruction would be practically sure. It was undoubtedly the emperor's intention to abandon the Rajput force to its fate, the moment it crossed the Indian border, withholding all support from Delhi; and if the Rajputs at all survived the incessant fighting in store for them and the rigours of the Afghan winter, they could on their way back to India be easily despatched by superior and fresh Mogal forces. It is extremely surprising that Jaswant Singh, usually so wary fell into the trap laid for him by the cunning emperor. Possibly an overweening confidence in himself might have induced him to accept the commission or he might have been deceived by the soft complimentary language of the other. Unquestionably Aurangzeb was a splendid student of human nature, and a past master in the art of dissimulation. He fully knew the vanities and susceptibilities of all his foes and how to manipulate them to his own advantage. This skill or statecraft, if it may be so called, enabled him to successfully tide over some of the most perilous crises in his career. Jaswant Singh and his contingents were given a hearty ovation at Delhi and a right royal send-off. Aurangzeb must have chuckled with mental satisfaction since his old foe was at last proceeding to his doom.

The campign proved to be a terrible one. Aurangzeb would not send the smallest succour either in men or materials, so that the ranks of the abandoned Rajput force in Afghanistan began to be dangerously thinned from day to day. Jaswant Singh had left his eldest son Pirthi Singh at Jodhpur, a young prince full of great promise. He was meanwhile invited to court by Aurangzeb. A poisoned robe of honour was smilingly bestowed on the innocent prince, which he was made to wear in the Darbar Hall. Within a couple of hours of his return Pirthi Singh expired in great agony. This news broke the hearts of his parents in the far away North. About the same time Jaswant Singh's other two sons, Jagat Singh and Dalthaman Singh, both children of tender age, died in the snows of Kabul due to exposure. On 10th December 1678, the emperor managed to have Jaswant Singh himself murdered by poison at Jamrud. And the same fine reward was meted out to the Mirza Raja of Amber for his meritorious services!

In February 1679 the Rathore queen, who was pregnant, gave birth to a posthumous son, named Ajit Singh, at Lahore, who now became the lodestar of all their drooping hopes. It was decided to return to Marwar. The queen and her dwindled escort, 250 men in all, had to pass through Delhi. They had yet to reckon with the emperor who wanted to seize the infant prince and made no secret of his intentions. The leaders of the escort were coerced, cajoled and offered enormous bribes if they would only deliver their infant lord. To his cruel mortification, however, the emperor learnt that the Rajputs were men of sterner mettle. "Arung offered to divide Maroo amongst them if they would surrender their prince; but they replied, 'our country is with our sinews and these can defend both it and our lord.'" The bold Rajputs had determined to foil the Mogal's infamous purpose by their desperate daring or perish in the attempt. Five thousand Mogal troops under Foulad Khan prepared to storm the Rajput encampment. The infant prince was dexterously carried out of the thickening danger by Mukand Das Khichi, while the Rajput ladies gladly immolated themselves on fire with the exception of the dowager queen. In the midst of her redoubtable warriors, headed by Durga Das Rathore, Raghunath Das Bhatti, Harnath Singh and Ranchhor Das, she then burst upon the besieging Mogals like a blast of lightning and literally hacked her way out through the streets of Delhi, hurling a glorious defiance at the heads of her cowardly assailants. Who could break the death-less determination of that dauntless Rajput band? The Mogals could not even dream that that battered handful of Rajputs would dare the seemingly superhuman task of attempting to break through their beleaguering cordons at the nerve centre of their mighty empire. The Rajput Sardars fought brilliant rearguard actions in this famous running battle against terrific odds and sacrificed their lives one after the other. The gallant Durga Das and Thakur Harnath Singh of Khimsar were among the very few who escaped alive, though covered all over with wounds and gore. Deeds of such marvellous heroism can scarcely be matched in any but Rajput history. The emperor was baulked of his prey.

Ajit Singh lived long enough to avenge the murder of his father and brother. In the 26 year's war of Rajput independence, which came on the heels of his escape from Delhi, he relentlessly carried fire and sword through Malwa, while yet in his teens. Valour was his inheritance. Later on, the machinations of the Syed brothers gave him another opportunity to wreak his vengeance on the house of Timur. After the battle of Sambhar in 1713 A. D. he made common cause with Syed Hussain Ali and in the assassination of the three successive Mogal emperors, during 1718 and 1719, he was the right hand partner of the two brothers.

# Chapter VI.

# Durga Das Rathore.

"Let his great example stand
Colossal seen of every land,
And keep the soldier firm, the statesman pure."

*Tennyson.*

About the close of 1605 A. D., a stalwart Rajput was leisurely riding by a smiling village of Marwar, one morning, when he descried a handsome maiden ascending the stone steps of a *Baori*, with a couple of heavy pitchers of water on her head. The matchless symmetry of her lithe young body, her natural grace and fair Aryan features bespoke good descent. She was unaware of the interest which her presence had aroused in the heart of the solitary horseman, who appeared to be transfixed with her majestic beauty. The Thakur had reined up his steed, and gazed after her long after she had passed out of his sight. He, Askaran Singh, the prime minister of Maharajah Jaswant Singh of Marwar, had fallen in love on the spot. That entrancing vision of loveliness was always present before his mind and gave him little rest. He longed to possess her and dreamt of what a fine race of children would result from their union. The Maharaja came to hear of this and before long the nuptials of Thakur Askaran Singh and his sweetheart were celebrated amidst great joy. The illustrious Durga Das Rathore was born of these parents in the year 1638 A. D. in the village of Salwa at a distance of 12 miles from Jodhpur. He inherited a powerful constitution and, like a true Rajput, became an adept in the use of arms in his very boyhood. His mother was a lady of uncommonly strong will, which led to domestic differences and eventually produced a permanent estrangement with her lord. Durga was barely 14 years of age when he and his mother were given a separate residence to live in at a distance of two miles from Salwa. Here the young Rathore grew up in seclusion under the elevating influence of his mother. She assiduously sowed the seeds of a hero in his boyish bosom. He developed a great passion for the chase and passed six uneventful years hunting the tiger, boar and other wild beasts in his native glens, until destiny came in one day to open the doors of the big world to the unknown Rajput lad.

Durga was passing by a neighbouring village pasture, where an altercation was going on between a villager and some of the state camel drivers who wanted to forcibly graze their camels on the village pasture land. It shortly led to blows and the camel drivers proceeded to belabour the poor villager who being unaided began to bleed. Durga could brook this cruel scene no longer. He expostulated with the camel drivers for their barbarity and tried to save the rustic. This humane action drew the wrath of the bullies on himself. The camel drivers felt slighted and got enraged. They let go the villager and assailed Durga Das with their stout bludgeons. The situation was desperate but the young Rathore proved himself to be more than a match for his ruffianly assailants. In the twinkling of an eye he had lodged a heavy fist on the temple of the nearest man, knocking him down senseless and snatched his bludgeon. The next instant he smashed the skull of the foremost villain, who fell stone dead. The rest of the camel drivers immediately took to their heels and reported the death of their comrade to the authorities. Durga was charged with murder and led before the Maharajah. It was however clearly established in the investigation which followed, that Durga had interfered with selfless motives to save the life of the poor villager, and was therefore honourably acquitted.

This adventure served to extricate Durga Das

from the obscurity of his village existence and gained him an introduction in the court circle. Maharajah Jaswant Singh was a great patron of merit. He not only appreciated the manly conduct of the young Rajput, but was so deeply impressed with his handsome bearing and frank avowal as to freely eulogise him before the courtiers. Somebody told the Maharajah that Durga Das was no other than the son of Thakur Askaran Singh, the prime minister, from his third wife. The Maharajah was so pleased as to send for Durga Das forthwith and took him on his personal staff. Soon after Jaswant Singh bestowed on him a valuable *jagir* near his paternal domain of Droonara on the Loni, as a further mark of royal favour.

Durga Das proved himself to be thoroughly deserving of the affection and esteem which the Maharajah bore him. That the young man developed into a redoubtable warrior is not surprising in view of the fact that the Rajput was a born fighter in that warlike age. The one great characteristic of Durga Das, however, which distinguished him above his fellows was the powerful restraint which he exercised over his speech and actions. He was fast developing rare traits of foresight and statesmanship. His valour which was unquestioned never degenerated into reckless impetuosity. The Maharajah naturally began to rely as much on his young protege's counsel as on his military prowess. And well it was that the keen intelligence of the great Rathore ruler had enabled him to single out this strong, vigilant and resourceful young man for a post of trust near his royal person.

Durga Das was barely 23 years of age when he had to depart for the Deccan with the Maharajah who was called upon to help Moazzam in prosecuting the war against Shivaji. For seven eventful years, thickly studded with adventures, the young Rathore attended on his beloved chief like his very shadow. To Durga Das' sleepless vigilance and matchless swordsmanship, the Maharajah owed his life more than once.

Maharajah Jaswant Singh became thoroughly disgusted with Aurangzeb's duplicity and returned to Marwar in 1670 A. D. Soon after Durga Das was chosen as ambassador to the court of Delhi. Aurangzeb's mind was ill at ease so long as the powerful ruler of Marwar continued to be suspicious and hostile. Aided by his extraordinary intelligence and tact, Durga Das was constantly trying to ease their strained relations so as to avoid actual armed conflict. He discharged his onerous duties with exemplary sagacity and success. His prolonged sojourn at Delhi gained him a thorough insight into the true nature of the Mogal's statecraft and political designs. Naturally endowed with a quick perception, he lost no opportunity of studying the court of Delhi at close quarters. He kept himself in touch with all the currents of Imperial ambition and intrigue which emanated from the capital and broke, at times with devestating effect, on distant countries bordering the Mogal empire. The knowledge thus acquired by Durga Das proved eventually to be a powerful bulwark of the liberties of Rajasthan.

In 1674 the Maharajah was invited to proceed to Kabul in order to quell the Afghan rebellion. Great promises of advancement were held out to him and he accepted the offer. Aurangzeb was delighted to learn these tidings, as he had deliberately planned the destruction of the great Rathore ruler, who had long been a thorn in his side. Durga Das was of course one of the notables who attended on the Maharajah. The Rathore contingents which proceeded to Kabul were cut off from all support from Delhi and abandoned to their fate. The rigours of the Afghan climate and campaign began to take a heavy toll of life and to crown the Rathores' woes, the Maharajah was poisoned at the instigation of Aurangzeb. It was thereupon decided to return to Marwar. How valiantly the widowed queen and her small escort, headed by Durga Das, fought their

way through Delhi to Marwar, has already been related in the previous chapter.

On reaching Marwar, Durga Das lost no time in ensuring the safety of his infant sovereign, who was taken to a Jain Monastry on the peak of Aboo, to be brought up in secrecy. The period of minority turned out to be bristling with dangers to the State. Attempts were successively made by the Eenods, the ancient rulers of Marwar, and Rao Ratan Singh a son of the celebrated Amar Singh Rathore, to oust the ruling family. The latter attempt was instigated by Aurangzeb himself. However the designs of the insurgents were frustrated on each occasion by the fidelity of the warlike clans headed by Durga Das. His selfless devotion to the interests of his infant sovereign was of too exalted a type to be overcome by the overtures of hostile adventurers, whether native or foreign.

The emperor Aurangzeb who was already smarting under a sense of shame at the escape of Ajit Singh from Delhi, was deeply galled at the failure of Rao Ratan. He wanted to enforce the *jazya* in Rajasthan and had long cherished a secret design for the forcible conversion of the Rajputs to Islam. Having recently achieved the murders of the Mirza Rajah and of Maharajah Jaswant Singh, the emperor considered it an opportune time for the fruition of his violent designs on Rajasthan. The choicest of the Mogal armies were therefore collected for the invasion of Marwar, for the ostensible object of punishing the Rathores for their defiant insolence. Durga Das, the soul of Rajput patriotism, was not idling. He was fully aware of all these warlike preparations and their sinister portent. The dowager queen of Marwar was a daughter of the illustrious house of the Maharana of Udaipur. As the hour of peril drew near, she appealed to the Maharana for succour. This led to the political union of the great Rathore and Seesodiya ruling houses and their dependant clans. Marwar and Mewar fully realised the gravity of the Mogal menace and determined to offer a deadly resistance to the common danger.

Aurangzeb started for Ajmer on the 9th January 1679, with a grand army numbering close upon one hundred thousand men, comprising formidable artillery served by Portuguese and French adventurers. The Rajputs could not with any hope of success give battle to this mighty host in the open field. The plains were therefore largely abandoned and the pivot of allied Rajput resistance was shifted to the Aravelli mountains. The Rathore contingents, led by the gallant Durga Das in person, began to closely cooperate with the Seesodiyas. The approaches to the

Aravellis were strengthened and a skilful plan of campaign was drawn up by the Rajput generals to entrap and destroy the foe in the hilly defiles. Even the native Bhils joined the Rajput forces to wage a patriotic war against the Mogal invaders. The emperor decided to strike a vital blow at Udaipur first and attacked it in such force that Durga Das considered it necessary to create a diversion. Accordingly he invaded Jhalore and the surprise was so surely planned that he carried fire and sword among the Mogal garrisons right up to the walls of Jodhpur, whose governor was obliged to pay a heavy ransom. Aurangzeb was constrained to turn back in order to save his garrisons in Marwar from the avenging steel of the infuriated Rathores. But the Mewar battalions led by prince Bhim Singh hung on the flanks of the retreating Mogals and harried them ceaselessly by night and day. At last the prince effected a junction with the Rathores operating in Godwar under Durga Das. A great battle was fought at Nadole at the close of 1681 A. D. in which the Mogals were completely defeated, though the heroic prince Bhim Singh fell fighting in the hour of victory. In this battle the combatants lost heavily on both sides. Thereupon prince Akbar, who felt sick of the war, sent over an embassy of peace to Durga Das. This proposal was naturally welcomed by the Rajputs but their diplomatic leader conceived of a finer plan for effecting the deliverance of Rajasthan.

Why should not Akbar seize the crown of India for himself with the help of the Rajputs and his own army ? The idea was splendid and easy of accomplishment. Aurangzeb, who was directing operations from Ajmer, could be captured before any reinforcements could be summoned to rush up to his assistance. Accordingly Akbar and Durga Das united to carry out the great design. But the coup was thwarted by the luxurious indolence of Akbar. Aurangzeb trembled for his safety but never lost his presence of mind. He caused a letter to fall into the hands of the Rajputs which made them suspect Akbar of treachery. The crafty emperor thus succeeded in sowing disunion among his enemies. The Rajputs, led by Durga Das, being completely deceived, marched off from the camp of Akbar. That luckless prince knew not what to do. Faced by dire misfortune, he threw himself on the generosity of Durga Das and prayed for sanctuary. At this juncture the emperor sent over a bribe of forty thousand gold *mohurs* to Durga Das with the request that he would hand over the fugitive Akbar. The Rajput leader was however proof against such temptations. He would not stoop to barter away his honour by turning traitor to the unhappy prince who had sought his sanctuary. The gold was not sent back by Durga Das. On the contrary it was seized and placed at the disposal of Akbar, in whose eyes tears of manly gratitude started at this signal act of devotion on the part of his protector. Aurangzeb was enraged and set in instant motion all his vast resources to catch his fugitive son. The desperate situation was however saved by Durga Das with consummate skill. To his eternal credit be it said that he dared the gravest dangers and distress in order to act up to his solemn pledge to Akbar.

"He holds no parley with unmanly fears;
Where duty bids, he confidently steers;
Faces a thousand dangers at her call,
And trusting in his God, surmounts them all."

*Wordsworth.*

Vigilant Mogal watchers were on the alert all over Marwar and doing their utmost to track down the rebel in order to earn the rich rewards promised by the emperor. Durga Das entrusted his elder brother, the fearless Sonag, with the conduct of the war against the Mogals and at the head of five hundred horse undertook to save Akbar and his family from the thickening dangers. So secretly was Akbar's family, composed of his youngwife, little children and a few attendants, conveyed to Durga Das' domain of Droonara by the faithful Rajput guides, that the ubiquitous Mogal spies failed to get the slightest inkling of their destination. Having thus ensured the safety and honour of the family, Durga Das set out with Akbar with a lighter heart to try conclusions with the Mogals.

A false scent was thrown out in the path of Aurangzeb, which carried him to Jhalore to his extreme chagrin and mortification. Meanwhile Durga Das, eluding Mogal outposts, was escorting his royal protege with incredible swiftness along the borders of Gujrat. He crossed the Dungarpur hills and boldly struck out on the road to Ahmadnagar. Here the Mogals were on the *qui vive.* Consequently Durga Das had to cautiously recede. A dash was then made through Banswara and eventually the whole party succeeded in crossing the Nerbudda without molestation. They proceeded to the court of Sambhaji and were welcomed at Raigarh in 1682 A. D. Soon after, Akbar, finding his position insecure, made good his escape to Persia.

Durga Das had daily opportunities at Raigarh of conferring with the Maratha patriots. It is needless to say that the weighty views exchanged at these historic meetings served to stiffen the resistance of the Rajput and Maratha patriots on either side in their defensive war against Aurangzeb.

While Durga Das was away in the Deccan. Sonagji carried on the war at home with extraordinary energy. The Mogals lost so heavily and were so hard pressed that the emperor was strongly advised by Asad Khan to make peace with the Rajputs. A treaty of peace was accordingly concluded and Aurangzeb, with his mind at ease, left for the Deccan. Before he started, however, he had bribed certain degenerates to poison the brave Sonag. This infamy having been achieved, the emperor declared the recent treaty as void. The Rajputs were enraged at the perfidy of their foes and resumed the war with redoubled fury. Young Tej Singh, a son of Durga Das, accompanied by a small batch of Rajputs, who had just arrived from the Deccan, took a brilliant part in the desultory cavalry fighting which followed. Bands of roving Rathores spread themselves over a vast country stretching from the environs of Agra right up to the borders of Sindh, raiding Mogal outposts, cutting down stragglers and supply trains. The roads of Malwa and Gujrat were also beset with elusive Rajput raiders, determined to harass the Mogals by ceaseless guerilla war. Durga Das himself returned from the Deccan in 1686, A. D. He persuaded the Yadavas of Bhanpura to cast in their lot with the national forces operating against the Mogals. The brave

Haras of Boondi also decided to unite with the Rathores. Thus was the Rajput resistance gathering momentum when Ajit Singh, the leige lord of Marwar, though yet a boy, emerged from his secret retreat on Aboo. His royal presence sent round an electric shock and stimulated the Rajputs to fresh exertions. They descended on Marwar like an irresistible avalanche; Mogal garrisons were put to the sword, the whole country was cleared of the foe and valuable booty was plundered. In 1690 A. D. Durga Das was hard at the heels of Saif Khan, the governor of Ajmer, pursuing him towards that city. During the next two years, however, the Mogals being heavily reinforced, regained most of their lost positions in Marwar and drove the Rathores back to the hills and their secret haunts in the desert.

The daughter of prince Akbar was entering maidenhood under the protection of Durga Das. This fact was a source of ceaseless anxiety to Aurangzeb, who feared lest Ajit Singh the youthful ruler of Marwar might catch a fancy for the beautiful Mogal princess. A fitful war and negotiations for her restoration followed. In 1695 Aurangzeb offered the highest honours of his court and enormous riches to Durga Das if he would restore the children of Akbar. The magnificence of the proferred bribe was sure to tempt had Durga Das possessed the slightest taint of selfishness. He was however the very soul of Rajput honour and disdainfully spurned the great prizes which the wily Mogal dangled before his gaze. Personal aggrandisement would oblige him to forsake the interests of his leige lord. The Mogal offer was coolly calculated to attain this object. Durga Das was well aware of Mogal statecraft to see through the artifice and without the slightest hesitation determined to sacrifice his personal interests before his duty to the boy Maharajah of Marwar. The Mogal viceroy of Gujrat, Shujat Khan, was lost in wonder and admiration when his ambassador brought back the refusal of the great Rathore warrior. Aurangzeb was growing anxious day by day and enquired the terms if any on which Durga Das would restore the princess. The latter had no mind to keep the princess as a hostage in Marwar and frankly offered to restore her in return for several districts of Marwar which were occupied by the Mogals. This proposal was eagerly accepted by the emperor in 1696 A. D. Akbar's children had been scrupulously brought up in the tenets of Islam in the desert castle of Droonara. On finding that they knew the Koran by heart, Aurangzeb was so thoroughly pleased with the honourable conduct of Duga Das as to confer on him the *jagir* of Dhanduka and several districts of Gujrat. Peace now reigned over the land for some years. In 1699 A. D. Durga Das persuaded the emperor te restore the districts of Jhalore and Sachore also to Maharajah Ajit Singh. It almost appears that Aurangzeb wanted to shower his favours on Durga Das with a view to destroy him at a convenient time. The latter was appointed governor of Patan in 1703 A. D. During the same year prince Azam, the successor of Shujat Khan, received secret instructions from the emperor to capture or kill Durga Das. Safdar Khan Babi was accordingy entrusted by the prince to carry out the emperor's orders. Durga Das was invited to attend the court at Ahmadabad. He came suspecting nothing and pitched his camp at Bareja on the Sabarmati. One of his trusty retainers who had had to go to Ahmadabad the same evening on a private errand, witnessed an unusual bustle in Azam's camp. A large array of mailed and gauntletted men-at-arms was moving about: military pickets were close at hand and appeared to be in readiness all around the place. In short the whole atmosphere was reeking with the preparations for some military enterprise. The Rajput pricked up his ears and gathered whatever information he could. He stole back at the dead of night to his camp on the Sabarmati and immediately acquainted his chief with the result of his lynx-eyed observations. Durga Das had enough intelligence to perceive that he had walked into a trap laid for him by the treacherous Mogals. Instantaneous flight alone could hold out any chance of escape as the Mogal spies were already prowling about the neighbourhood. The Rajputs silently struck their tents and galloped off on the wings of haste. However the flight was immediately discovered and several Mogal squadrons set off in hot pursuit. As the Babis were bearing down on the Rajput party, the grandson of Durga Das volunteered with a few followers to cover the flight. He gallantly charged the pursuers and with his followers fell fighting against tremendous odds. His heroic self-sacrifice was not in vain; the rest of the Rajput band made good their escape. Durga Das headed straight for Patan. From there he took his family and proceeded to Tharad. Marwar was soon reached, where Durga Das rested awhile after his recent toilsome marches.

At this time the plains towns of Marwar were occupied by the Mogals, who committed all sorts of excesses therein. The Rathores maintained their independence in the hills and on the confines of the great desert, where the Mogals dared not follow them. A state of war prevailed but no decisive movement was afoot. As a matter of fact the Mogal pressure on Marwar had considerably slackened owing to their complicated military undertakings in the Deccan and elsewhere, which required to be fed by constant drafts from all parts of the empire. The Maratha menace was multiplying in sinister proportions. Gujrat lay in imminent danger of Maratha invasion. In Marwar therefore the Rathore position grew stronger in proportion to the growth of the Mogals' troubles and travails in other parts of the country. Maharajah Ajit Singh and Durga Das were cautiously biding time until the hour of vengeance drew near. In 1705 A. D. Prince Bedar Bakht the viceroy received the disconcerting news that Verishalji of Rajpipla and Ajit Singh were simultaneously preparing to shake off the Mogal yoke. Tharad was captured and sacked by the Rathores after a surprise attack, and before the Mogals had time to assemble in strength, the town was as swiftly quitted. Shah Quli, a son of Kazim Beg, the governor of Jodhpur, who was travelling towards Patan to take up his new appeintment as Deputy Governor there, fell in with Durga Das who was marching on Marwar. Durga Das forthwith attacked the Mogal and slew him with all his men.

Immediately after this exploit news arrived that

Masum Quli, the governor of Viramgaon, was arriving, bound south. An ambush was therefore laid by Durga Das at Chaniar in the Chunval. The Mogals came on trotting jauntily when the Rajputs pounced on them from opposite sides. Terror struck, the Mogal escort fled, leaving large numbers on the field. Masum Quli escaped with a couple of wounds as momentoes of the ambuscade. By forced marches then Durga Das penetrated the heart of Marwar and inflicted a heavy defeat on the Mogals in open battle near his castle of Droonara about the close of 1705 A. D. The next two years brought continuous misfortune to the Mogals. The Rathores relentlessly pursued them from place to place capturing enormous quantities of war material and the accumulated wealth which the Mogals had ravished from the country. Immediately on receipt of the welcome news of Aurangzeb's death in 1707 A. D., Maharajah Ajit Singh began his irresistible march on Jodhpur. Kunwar Mohkam Singh who tried to oppose the advance, was defeated. Jodhpur was surrendered by Jafar Quli, a son of Kazim Beg, without striking a blow in defence; this marked the close of Mogal occupation of Marwar. The war eventually ended in August 1709, when a treaty of amity and friendship was concluded between Ajit Singh and the reigning Mogal emperor.

The peerless virtues of Durga Das had won him many foes in the court of Ajit Singh, who appears to have been misled by their organized campaign of slander. It is a thousand pities that such a gallant preserver of his king and country, fell into royal disfavour owing to the machinations of his jealous enemies. An indescribable sadness thus overspread the evening of Durga Das' noble life. His enemies went so for as to depute eight horsemen to murder him on a highway near Narnaul. The dastardly assassins attacked the aged warrior about dusk. Out flashed the gleaming blade of Durga Das and he closed in mortal combat with the cowardly hirelings. Age had neither impaired the agility of his mighty frame nor dimmed the fire of his eagle eyes. His assailants were almost appalled by his exhibition of superhuman strength and skill in swordsmanship, for they fell mortally wounded one after the other until only one poor wretch remained. Durga Das could have killed him outright but decided to spare his life. The wretch was thrown from his horse and began to cower in abject terror. Durga Das coolly dismounted and cut off the man's ears, who disclosed the plot at the point of the victor's sword. Maharajah Ajit Singh was in a fearful fix. On the one hand he wished to favour the heroic protector of his infancy, while on the other he had to reckon against the organized opposition of his other Sardars. He was eventually constrained to conciliate the latter. As soon as Durga Das learnt this fateful news, he decided to go into voluntary exile from the beloved land of his birth. Accompanied by his family and private retainers he proceeded to the court of Maharana Amar Singh of Mewar, who bestowed on his illustrious guest the *parganah* of Rampur and a princely pension. There the aged hero of Marwar passed the remnant of his mortal days in peace, until, in 1711, he quitted this ungrateful world to take up his rightful place in the Valhalla of human valour.

> "He was a man, take him for all in all,
> I shall not look upon his like again."
>
> *Shakespeare.*

# Chapter VII.

# Shivaji.

"Borne on your daring pinions soar sublime
Above the shoal and eddy of the Time."

*Schiller.*

Strange as it may seem, it was a scion of the royal Seesodia house of Chittor who was destined to be a scourge of the Mogals and lay deep the foundations of a power which finally wrested from them the sovereignty of Hindustan. After experiencing various vicissitudes of fortune, the descendents of prince Ajey Singh, who had escaped from the doom which befell Chittor at the close of the 13th century, had settled down in the uplands of Maharashtra and adopted the family name of Bhonsla.

Shivaji was born in this family on 10th April 1627, of Shahaji and Jijabai. Shahaji was one of the principal nobles of the Bijapur kingdom and had won great renown as a military commander in the interminable wars which the Mogals carried on against the Deccan sultanates. As he emerged into his very boyhood, Shivaji evinced a spirited, enterprising and thoughtful disposition. It was proposed to solemnize his marriage in 1640 at Bijapur with a girl of the ancient Nimbalkar family, but Shivaji vehemently protested against these ceremonies being conducted at the capital of a Mahomedan state, where, he apprehended, the religious rites might be obstructed and restrictions, obnoxious to his soul, would have to be faced. The marriage was therefore celebrated at Poona in compliance with his wishes. Scenes of cow slaughter were particularly hateful to Shivaji. His sojourn in Bijapur caused him continual mental torture and he resolved to quit the city. The Sultan was prevailed upon by Shahaji, with the valuable assistance of Mir Jumla, to prohibit cow slaughter within the city walls. A few days after the promulgation of this *firman* Shivaji, while riding by, came across a butcher who broke it, and promptly cut him down.

Bijapur soon grew too hot a place for the young Maratha with his violent tendencies and ready sword. While hating the religious persecution, to which the Hindus were subjected in Bijapur, Shivaji had laid by a vast store of military and administrative knowledge in his receptive brains. There were ominous murmurs within Bijapur of the lad's uncontrolled excesses and Shahaji was obliged in his own interests to send him away to the family Jagir at Poona in charge of Dadaji Kcndadev, the faithful Brahmin secretary.

Shivaji had freer play for his genius in the wild atmosphere of his native mountains. He used to listen with rapt attention to all the tales of the greatest heroes of Hindu legend which his mother Jijabai related to him. These filial discourses instilled a passionate love of liberty and yearning for adventure into Shivaji's heart. His military education was ably looked after by Dadaji Kondadev who also initiated his youthful protege into the arts of practical administration. On the death of Kondadev, Shivaji took over the administration of the family estates in person. Now he began to come in close contact with the native Mavalis and earn their eternal friendship by his personal magnetism. The family Jagir comprised the districts of Poona, Supa and Maval. The authority of the Nizamshahi and latterly of the Bijapur dynasty had been at best precariously exercised over these hilly regions; nor did the Hindu populace relish it when it was enforced. Accordingly the advent of Shivaji with his patriotic tendencies and chivalrous motives was hailed with joy at the birth of a new hope. As a matter of fact the Western Ghats never seriously acknowledged the supremacy of Bijapur nor were the hill forts strongly garrisoned.

In 1646, Shivaji began to translate his resolve to uproot the supremacy of Islam into action. He despatched his Mavali retainers to the fort of Torna, twenty miles to the south of Poona, to persuade its governor to hand over the fort. The latter was easily bribed to acquiesce into the proposal. While the fortifications of this fort were being renewed, a buried treasure was discovered with which Shivaji built a new fort named Rajgarh. He now began to seize one hill fort after another. The forts of Chakan, Shivner, Singhgarh, Purandhar and Visapur were thus captured. So far, however, not a drop of blood had been shed as all these forts had been seized by strategem or persuasion. The Bijapur authorities had not therefore found much cause for alarm. One of Shivaji's most daring comrades, Tanaji Malusray, plundered a convoy of treasure which had been sent to Bijapur by Mulla Ahmad, the governor of Kalyan. This led to the outbreak of hostilities. A Maratha force under Abaji Sondev swooped down on Kalyan and sacked the town; Mulla Ahmad's daughter was also taken prisoner. The maiden, a vision of dazzling beauty, was produced by Abaji in Shivaji's court as a prize of war. However Shivaji treated her as his own daughter and honourably sent her back to her father at Bijapur under safe escort.

One of the foremost factors which lay at the root of Shivaji's career of unbroken triumph was his intimate knowledge of the Maratha country, its glens and valleys, roads and hill paths as well as the actual strength of each fort. His spies were spread all over the country. They boldly enlisted themselves in enemy garrisons; at times they managed to enter hostile forts by carrying bundles of fodder in supply trains. The master mind of Shivaji was continually directing these secret activities and he soon reaped the full harvest of these toilsome preparations. The capture of numerous forts like Lohgarh, Tikoni, Kelna and Ghangad was conveniently effected. The fortifications of Rairee were strengthened and the fort of Raigarh was built on the plateau of the hill. During an expedition into the Konkans the famous sword named "Bhawani" was presented to Shivaji by Gawalkar Sawant, a Maratha chief, who was anxious to propitiate Shivaji and enter his service. After a neat religious ceremony of consecration to the goddess Bhawani, Shivaji grasped the sword as an omen of victory in the future.

A series of acts of open hostility had at last roused the indignation of the Bijapur Government. As every protest failed to check Shivaji in the prosecution of his grave designs, his father Shahaji was imprisoned at Bijapur and the Sultan threatened to close the last aperture in his prison if Shivaji did not surrender the captured forts within a specified time. In this fateful crisis Shivaji appealed to Shah Jahan offering to enter Mogal service if his father could be liberated by the emperor's intercession. Shah Jahan acceded to this proposal and sent an order to Adil Shah of Bijapur to liberate Shahaji, threatening dire consequences in case of non-compliance. The Sultan complied and Shahaji was set at liberty but was obliged to remain in Bijapur, for four years. During this period of enforced inactivity Shivaji consolidated his possessions, made revenue settlements and gave the blessings of peace to his people.

Since Shivaji had conciliated Shah Jahan, he was anxious that the former should attend the court and accept a rank in the Mogal army. However Shivaji offered various excuses and entered into negotiations with Murad to prolong the issue. In 1657, Shah Jahan deputed Aurangzeb and Mir Jumla to conquer the Bijapur kingdom. Shivaji proposed to aid the Mogals in the conquest of the Konkan sea-board if he were guaranteed in his possessions. To this Aurangzeb readily agreed. Sometime ago Shivaji had laid claim to the possession of Junnar and Ahmadnagar which had been rejected by the emperor. Now that the Mogals were busy in the war against

Bijapur, Shivaji snatched the opportunity to rush and sack the two towns. He brought back a great treasure, over a thousand horses and several elephants as loot of war to the fort of Rajgarh. He now reorganized his cavalry under daring captains of whom Netaji Palkar was a renowned one.

Luckily for Shivaji, Aurangzeb received news from the capital of his father's illness and hurried to the north after concluding a hasty peace with Bijapur. Shivaji thus escaped the penalty which he would have had to pay for his attacks on Junnar and Ahmadnagar. He took care however to send an apology for these encroachments.

For some time Shivaji had felt that the More chief of the Westerm Ghats was a thorn in his side who withstood Shivaji's domination over that part of the country. Shivaji had therefore recourse to strategem. The chief, a loyal feudatory of Bijapur, was invited to a conference and assassinated by Shivaji's men; after a grim fight all resistance was overcome. Javli the capital of the Mores with all their hill forts passed into Shivaji's hands.

The hill fort of Rohida was next surprised during the night. Its brave chief Bandal fell fighting and his followers submitted, out of whom Baji Prabhu gained lasting glory later on in the service of Shivaji. The fort of Pratapgarh was built under the directions of Moroji Pingle. Shivaji conquered a number of towns on the Konkan sea-board. He enlisted a force of 700 Pathans who had been disbanded by the Bijapur authorities and put them under the command of Ragho Ballal Atre.

The court of Bijapur was thoroughly incensed by Shivaji's ceaseless depredations. Aurangzeb was busy fighting his brothers in Hindustan and could not therefore be expected to intimidate Bijapur if a sharp lesson were taught to Shivaji. Accordingly Afzal Khan the most famous general of the kingdom was chosen by Ali Adil Shah for the purpose, with express orders by the queen-mother to entrap or kill Shivaji, by fair means or foul. The general marched a powerful army comprising artillery and a camel corps through Shivaji's territories and desecrated all the famous temples of Tuljapur, Pandharpur and Shingnapur. His soldiery murdered several Brahmins and slaughtered kine in the temples. Meanwhile the Maratha leader was not idle. He stationed himself in the fort of Pratapgarh, thoroughly stocked it with provisions and invoked divine guidance and the blessings of his mother. Tradition has it that his tutelary goddess Bhawani visited Shivaji in a dream, exhorted him to wreak vengeance on the invaders for desecrating the sacred shrines and assured him of victory. Never for a moment, however, Shivaji made light of the peril which confronted him and his young state. On the contrary Afzal Khan openly bragged that he would capture Shivaji and parade him in chains through the streets of Bijapur to crown his triumph. Shivaji was kept closely informed of Afzal Khan's movements, the strength and dispositions of his forces by skilful Maratha spies, of whom Wishwas Rao used to penetrate into every part of the Mahomedan encampment in the garb of a mendicant. On the nearer approach of Afzal Khan, Shivaji assumed an air of abject penitence and opened negotiations in a strain of humiliation. If the Khan would intercede for his pardon by the Sultan of Bijapur, Shivaji was ready to pay his respects to such an invincible general. The vanity of Afzal Khan was tickled by the apparent submissiveness of the Maratha and he agreed to meet Shivaji half way up the hill of Pratapgarh with a small escort. The main body of the Mahomedan army was left at Jowly, the base of the hill, without any precautions having been taken against a possible ambuscade, which the Maratha had carefully planned. Under the dense undergrowth and thick foliage of the surrounding jungle lay hid picked Mavali forces under the command of Netaji Palkar and Moroji Pingle two of the finest Maratha captains, ready to fall on the Mahomedan army at a moment's notice.

After performing his ablutions Shivaji devoutly offered a prayer at the altar of his guardian goddess for the success of his enterprise. It was death or victory to him, knowing as he did the treacherous and fanatical character of his foes. Jijabai suppressed the swelling emotions of her heart as Shivaji started for the meeting and blessed him with an augury of success. Afzal Khan had already arrived at the pavilion which had been erected for the meeting, armed with a sword and attended by Sayyad Banda, a redoubtable swordsman of the Deccan. Shivaji had taken the precaution to wear a jacket of chain mail under his coat; he also carried a weapon called the Bagh-nakh ( the tiger's claws ) on the fingers of his left hand. Whether Afzal Khan or Shivaji struck the first blow will never be definitely known, as historians have differed very widely in their verdict on this point. Suffice it to say that Shivaji thrust his tiger's claws deep into the entrails of the burly Khan and drew them out. Jiva Mahalya a retainer of Shivaji, pounced on Sayyad Banda and lopped off his right arm at the shoulder blade. A brief melee ensued in which Tanaji Malusray cut off Afzal Khan's head and fixed it on a lance. In accordance with pre-arranged signals, a bugle was sounded from the pavilion to convey tidings of success to the garrison of the fort who in their turn fired a cannon. Thereupon the Marathas lying in ambush fell upon the Bijapur army sword in hand and slew several hundreds who showed fight. Shivaji had however given strict orders not to kill the Mahomedan soldiery while they ran. The rout was complete. The lives of hundreds who surrendered were spared by the generous victor. Fazal Khan, the son of the erstwhile proud general, had escaped while wounded by bribing Khandoji, a Mavali leader. When Shivaji came to know of this, he had Khandoji executed for his treachery.

All the rich martial equipment of the Bijapur army comprising 7000 horses, hundreds of camels and elephants, field artillery, several lakhs of rupees worth of gold and silver and pearls, and the entire camp fell into the hands of the Marathas. What Shivaji gained more than all this sudden acquisition of material resources was the moral support of his countrymen. Maharashtra was thrilled to the core at this magnificent exploit and broke out into universal jubilations. Shivaji's enterprise was stamped with the national character and he was openly hailed as the champion of Hinduism. From all over the Deccan bands of bold Maratha soldiers flocked to serve under his victorious banners. The heart of every Maratha worth his salt was overflowing with pride and enthusiasm. Shivaji's career of victory was crowned with success in other directions as well. The forts of Panhala, Vishalgarh, Basantgarh, Rangna and a host of smaller fortresses on the crest of the Sahyadri range were captured by him.

The disaster which overtook Afzal Khan's army caused serious consternation in Bijapur. For several days vague alarms were afloat that Shivaji was rushing up with his legions to sack the Mahomedan capital. The Sultan and his mother were beside themselves with grief and impotent rage. Not one of the court nobles was inclined to undertake another offensive against the dreaded Maratha warrior. At last the Sultan was obliged to conciliate Sidi Johar, a powerful Abyssinian nobleman who had since some time become estranged with him, in order to rehabilitate the prestige of the Bijapur government. Accompanied by Fazal Khan, who was burning with the desire of revenge for his father's death, Sidi Johar led a more powerful army than before against Shivaji and besieged him in the fort of Panhala. The siege dragged into several months. Shivaji became anxious to escape in order to conduct the operations in other theatres of war and soon gave the silp to the besiegers. But the escape was forthwith discovered and a strong force under Fazal Khan set out in pursuit. To ensure the safety of his flight towards Vishalgarh, Shivaji realised that it was necessary to hold the pursuers at bay. A small Mavali troop under Baji Prabhu was therefore stationed at a hilly defile, through which the pursuers had to pass. Bravely did this small band defend the passage of the dangerous defile. Wave after wave of Mahomedan attack broke on their stout phalanx. At last the booming of five cannon shots from the fort of Vishalgarh announced to friend and foe that Shivaji had safely reached his destination. By then that immortal fight was over. Baji Prabhu, the heroe of the Pass, was mortally wounded in the very moment of his king's triumph; his body was carried away by the remnant of the Mavalis who struck out into the dense jungle paths where the Mahomedans dared not follow them.

Sidi Johar failed to capture the fort of Panhala which was ably defended by Raghunath Ballal, while the elusive Maratha light horse under Netaji Palkar worried the Sidi day and night by their intensive guerilla war. It was soon realised by the Sidi that his campaign had proved a futile one. 'He had gained very little appreciable ground, had suffered considerable losses in men and had lost the morale of his army, who clamoured to be led back before the fearful rains, which were about to burst, caught them in the Ghats country. Accordingly Sidi Johar had no alternative but to lead back his dispirited army to Bijapur where he was bitterly upbraided by Ali Adil Shah on his failure.

The Sultan now took the field in person with an overwhelming army at his back and gained some initial advantages but he was obliged to canton his army outside the Ghats owing to the outbreak of the monsoon. This however proved no deterrant to Shivaji who found time to punish the Sawant of Wadi and the chief of Mudhol who had all along actively aided the Bijapur Government. Both of these chiefs were killed in battle and their capitals were stormed and sacked. Like forked lightning Shivaji next overran the Portuguese territories carrying fire and sword right up to the gates of Goa. There was no alternative for the Portuguese Government but to sue for peace which was concluded on their agreeing to pay a large annual tribute in gold and cannon. These brilliant successes as well as news of rebellion in the southern provinces served to depress the spirits of the Sultan to such an extent that in 1662 he made peace with Shivaji. The Sultan recognised Shivaji as independent ruler of the territories conquered by him and agreed to pay him an annual tribute of Rupees 35 lakhs.

Meanwhile Aurangzeb had secured the Peacock Throne at Delhi. He was seriously perturbed at the news of Shivaji's stirring exploits in the Konkans. The birth of a new power in the fastnesses of the Western Ghats which had successfully defied the armies of Bijapur struck a note of alarm in the mind of the Mogal emperor. Moreover Shivaji had not hesitated from ravaging Mogal territories along the border whenever it suited his purpose. Accordingly Aurangzeb deputed his uncle Shaista Khan, the viceroy of the Deccan, to reduce the forts of Shivaji and capture all the territories which had been conquered by him. In 1660, Shaista Khan began an irresistible march over the plains country and stationed himself at Poona. He next attacked the fort of Chakan of which the governor bravely held out against the Mogals for more than two months. Shivaji gave the Mogals a good taste of his inimitable tactics in war. They were harassed by clouds of light Maratha horse, under Netaji Palkar and Moroji Pingle who ravaged the Mogal districts of Ahmadnagar and Aurangabad with fire and sword. Maratha attacks developed like the whirlwind in the most unexpected quarters and by the time the Mogals turned out to intercept them the raiders were gone. Shivaji laid siege to the fort of Prabalgarh and captured it

Shaista Khan was obliged to ask the emperor for reinforcements as the task of breaking up Maratha power proved to be a harder nut to crack than he had imagined. A fresh army under Maharaja Jaswant Singh of Jodhpur therefore arrived to aid him. It appears that Shivaji succeeded in enlisting the secret sympathies of the great Rajput chief in his own sacred cause. One night Shivaji and a choice band of his bravest warriors, inviegled themselves with a marriage party into Poona and soon made their way into Shaista Khan's palace. As soon as their presence was discovered an alarm was given and Shaista Khan saved his life by jumping through a window, although not before Shivaji had cut down some fingers of his hand. However the Khan's son and followers were all slaughtered on the spot. Shivaji and his men made good their escape from Poona in the wild uproar and confusion which ensued in the town. A half hearted pursuit followed but Shivaji safely reached the fort of Singhgarh, at the foot of which hundreds of the Mogals were mowed down by well directed gun fire from the battlements above. The Mogals returned to Poona beaten and crestfallen, harried by swarms of Maratha horsemen. This sparkling adventure took place in 1663 and struck the death bearded in his own den by his wily Maratha adversary inspite of all his vast military concentration and precautions at Poona. He smelt treachery in his own camp. It almost appeared as if nothing was impossible for Shivaji to accomplish. Aurangzeb despatched Prince Moazzam to relieve the disgraced Khan in his viceroyalty of the Deccan and transferred him to far away Bengal.

To avenge the occupation of Poona by Shaista Khan, Shivaji determined to sack the famous Mogal port of Surat. In January 1664, he swooped down on Surat and pillaged it for three days without the slightest opposition from its Mogal governor, who shut himself in the castle out of sheer fright and sent out repeated appeals to Aurangzeb for succour. Shivaji stripped the wealthy merchants of this flourishing harbour, the largest emporium of trade in the Middle East and the centre of pilgrim traffic to the holy places of Islam, of their fabulous riches. It is estimated that his total haul amounted to over two crores of rupees. Although the majority of the wealthy inhabitants were forced to disgorge their hoards at the point of the sword, yet Shivaji had the generosity to spare and protect several of them. Bernier in his Travels says "During the pillage of Surat, Sevagi respected the habitation of the Reverend Father Ambrose, the Capuchin missionary.

'The Frankish padres are good men' said he 'and shall not be molested.' He spared also the house of a deceased Delale or Gentile Broker of the Dutch because assured that he had been very charitable while alive." This frank testimony makes it all too evident that the heart of Shivaji was overflowing with the milk of human sympathy in the midst of his most blood curdling adventures.

Aurangzeb was naturally furious when he learnt of this outrage. That Shivaji had plundered even the pilgrim ships bound for Mecca, gave a keener edge to the emperor's bitterness and he vowed revenge against the former. Maharaja Jai Singh was despatched to the Deccan in 1665 to destroy Shivaji. Apparently Aurangzeb was labouring under a strange delusion about the resources and fighting strength of the Maratha chief, which he greatly underrated. The Mogals who expected an easy march over the Maratha country were staggered by the stout resistance offered to them at every step. For several months they failed to capture the rocky fort of Purandhar which was defended by Morar Baji with the utmost gallantry against overwhelming odds. The siege of the fort of Singhgarh met with as little success.

Jai Singh soon realised the immensity of the task before him. He was undoubtedly one of the finest diplomats of Aurangzeb's court. Rather than prolong a dubious and dangerous war, he obtained the emperor's permission to open negotiations with Shivaji and persuaded him to acknowledge the suzerainty of the Mogals. Jai Singh also prevailed upon him to visit the emperor and pledged his Rajput honour for his safety at the capital. Accordingly on the eve of his fateful journey to Agra, Shivaji assembled all his Sardars in the fort of Raigarh and made suitable arrangements for the administration of his country during his absence. As the day of departure dawned, Shivaji performed his ablutions and invoked the protection of the goddess Bhawani, his tutelary deity. Jijabai gave him her fervent benedictions. And Shivaji turned his back on Maharashtra to face the Great Mogal in the North.

On reaching Agra, Shivaji was received by Ram Singh, a son of Jai Singh, and another Mogal grandee. The court as well as the Zenana was agog with excitement to behold such a celebrated person. An awful scene took place in the Darbar when Shivaji was presented. He lost his temper when assigned a place in the second row of courtiers and insulted the emperor, who, however, maintained a calm exterior and directed Ram Singh to take away the incensed Maratha from the Darbar Hall. The situation grew tenser in the days which followed. A powerful guard was put around Shivaji's residence so that he virtually found himself a prisoner.

> "Still in his stern and self-collected mien,
> A conqueror's more than captive's air is seen."
>
> *Byron.*

He began to exercise his fertile genius at this supreme crisis of his life to invent a plan of escape. He cultivated friendly relations with the Mogal nobility and started sending them presents of sweetmeats in huge baskets which had been procured for the purpose. It took him several months before he succeeded in throwing his enemies completely off their guard. One evening the soldiers of the guard were struck by the unusual silence which reigned in Shivaji's apartments and on venturing in were horror stricken to find that he had escaped. Aurangzeb raved with fury on receipt of this news. Mogal forces scoured the country far and wide over all the roads leading to the Deccan in the vain attempt to catch the Maratha eagle. But Shivaji had taken an eastern route towards Puri via Muttra and Benares, in the garb of a *sannyasi* to escape detection. After a multitude of petty adventures, he safely reached Maharashtra to the boundless joy of his people. It is probable that Ram Singh connived at Shivaji's escape from Agra as Aurangzeb had openly broken faith with his father by threatening Shivaji into submission and keeping him in close confinement at the capital. For how could the noble Rajputs, father and son, contemplate this perfidy and whatever else lurked at the back of the emperor's mind, with passive indifference ?

On his safe return to the Deccan, Shivaji declared war on the treacherous Mogals whom he vowed never to trust again. His minister Moroji Pingle had already taken a number of forts which had been ceded by Shivaji to Jai Singh. But the strategic forts of Singhgarh and Purandhar still remained in Mogal occupation. About this time, in 1668, Moazzam who commanded the Mogal armies in the Deccan feigned a rebellion against the emperor and invoked the aid of Shivaji. However the latter was not to be trapped a second time. The sham rebellion soon fizzled out and completely justified the caution of the wary Maratha leader. Shivaji launched a powerful offensive against the Bijapur and Golconda kingdoms and forced them to pay heavy tribute to escape molestation in the future. The fact is that their courtiers were no better than gilded popinjays incapable of initiative, while their blustering generals were afraid to take the field against the daring and warlike Marathas with their rough and ready efficiency and confounding mobility. Aurangzeb was more than ever alarmed at the rapid extension of

Maratha conquests in the Peninsula and resolved to launch a fresh offensive against them. Shivaji decided to strike the first blow himself. The fort of Singhgarh was held in great strength by a veteran Rajput warrior named Udai Bhan on behalf of the Mogals. Tanaji Malusray, one of the bravest Maratha captains, volunteered to capture this fort with the help of a picked Mavali force. Accordingly on a dark night in February 1670, Tanaji scaled the rocky walls of the fort with his chosen comrades and surprised the garrison. The Rajputs fought bravely. Their leader rushed into the thickest of the fight and singled out the gigantic Maratha leader whose mighty strokes were dealing destruction right and left. The duel between Tanaji and Udai Bhan was terrific but brief. They were acknowledged masters in the art of swordsmanship and soon both fell mortally wounded. The Mavalis overcame the resistance of the garrison and at daybreak the ochre-coloured banner of Shivaji waved triumphantly over the battlements of the fort of Singhgarh. The forts of Purandhar and Shivner were also wrested from the Mogals. Surat was stormed and sacked a second time.

Fresh Mogal armies arrived under Mahabat Khan to weigh down the balance of war against the Marathas. In 1672 a large force under Ikhlas Khan advanced to lay siege to the fort of Salheri. Shivaji, who realised the strategic importance of this fort, gave battle to the Mogal host under the walls of the fort and inflicted a crushing defeat on them. Five thousand of the Mogals lay dead on the battlefield; their leader Ikhlas Khan was taken prisoner. The casualties on the Maratha side amounted to less than 1500 men. The victors captured a vast hoard of war material, comprising gold and silver bullion, horses, elephants, camps and kettledrums. Soon afterwards, Hambirrao gained a splendid victory over a Bijapur army under Abdul Karim near the fort of Panhala. Inspite of his victory Shivaji was sad at the loss of Pratap Rao Gujar, one of his ablest generals, who fell fighting valiantly in this battle. Tireless military activity marked the conduct of Shivaji at this period. Having beaten back the best of the Mogals in war as in statecraft, Shivaji found little difficulty in ravaging the territories of the Deccan Sultans and levying *Chouth* by force of arms.

Time had now arrived when Shivaji decided to assume the insignia of royalty. As the Brahmans of Maharashtra raised some theological objections, he was advised to invite Ganga Bhat, the most learned and celebrated Brahmin scholar of Benares, to his court at Raigarh, where in open debate he quashed all objections by means of his superior learning. In the midst of scenes of unrivalled splendour Shivaji was crowned at Raigarh on 6th June 1674 after the performance of elaborate ritual as enjoined by the Shastras. This consummate glory of his triumphant career was formally proclaimed by cannon fire at an appointed hour from the numerous forts which bristled over Shivaji's dominions.

> "Something mighty and sublime
> Leave behind to conquer time;
> Glorious 'tis to live for aye,
> When these forms have pass'd away."
>
> *Goethe.*

As the Maratha chroniclers state, Ganga Bhat declared "By getting yourself formally crowned you will complete the humiliation of Aurangzeb and the other Sultans" : this prophesy foretold a correct index of the minds of Shivaji's contemporary Mahomedan potentates. That the Maratha champion after setting up as an independent Hindu power in the Deccan should consecrate his reign by the sanction of religion was gall and wormwood to the soul of Aurangzeb.

Under orders from the emperor the Mogals undertook another offensive against the Marathas. Shivaji deputed his trusty general Hambirrao to carry the war into the Mogal territories in the north.

Shivaji

This formidable warrior, a true disciple of Shivaji in the art of guerilla war, suddenly appeared in the Broach district and began to lay waste the country. His swift strokes spread consternation and terror in the province of Gujrat. The diversion thus created forced the Mogals to retire from the Maratha country. While these events were happening in the north, Moroji Pingle rushed on Bassein and forced the Portuguese Government to yeild *Chowth* at the point of the sword. In May 1675, Shivaji reduced the fort of Phonda and put the entire garrison, including its governor Mahomed Khan, to the sword. In short Shivaji's victorious squadrons overran the whole country up to the borders of Kanara and a new chain of fortifications along the borders of the Bijapur kingdom was built in order to maintain a firm grip over the conquered territory. Next year Shivaji led an expedition to invade the Karnatik. The Sultan of Golconda was in such a state of terror on the near approach of the Maratha army that he agreed to pay heavily towards the expenses of the expeditionary force, with the utmost alacrity. Shivaji paid a visit to the Sultan at his capital and was lavishly treated. After a round of royal entertainments, Shivaji left Bhagnagar and invaded the Karnatik. He soon captured the forts of Gingi and Vellore and placed them under the command of loyal Maratha captains. These successes and the havoc wrought by the other Maratha squadrons operating in the Dravid country caused repeated flutters of alarm in Madras and its English Colony. News of another impending Mogal invasion having arrived, Shivaji returned to the Konkans to cope with whatever situation might arise.

The Mogals were at this time vigorously endeavouring to subvert the Deccan Sultanates. Mussaoud Khan the prime minister of Bijapur appealed to Shivaji for succour, which the latter was only too glad to ofter. The valuable assistance rendered by the Maratha army enabled the Sultan of Bijapur to roll back the tide of Mogal invasion. He compensated these timely services by permanently ceding several fertile districts in the Peninsula to Shivaji. The closing years of Shivaji's life were distinguished by his ceaseless efforts to uproot the maritime power of the Sidis of Janjira. He had the sagacity to found a strong navy of his own to protect the seaboard of his kingdom which was open to the attacks of the seafaring Abyssinians. Janjira was more than once invested and bombarded by the navy and land batteries of Shivaji. The war with the Sidis was a protracted struggle in which the British at Bombay a treaty of mutual friendship between the British and Shivaji was concluded in the early part of 1680.

Soon after the great Maratha ruler lay on his death-bed. The tremendous strain of forced marches, hard fighting and the constant alarms of war at last broke down his iron constitution. Having realised that the end of his mortal career was near, Shivaji calmly settled the affairs of his kingdom which he entrusted to the care of his veteran officers, generals, statesmen and administrators, whose loyal labours had helped him to hammer the neighbouring Sultanates and set up a powerful Hindu monarchy on their ruins.

> "How blest are they who sink to rest
> With all their country's wishes blest!"
>
> *Collins.*

Has the cold hand of Time served to dim the glory of the departed hero, his sublime ideals, iron will, deep political understanding and mastery of the art of war? No. On the contrary time has served to dissipate the clouds of suspicion and base accusation which had been let loose over Shivaji's fame by the impotent revilings of his discomfited adversaries, their henchmen and later-day sympathisers. Their mendacious narratives which bear the unmistakeable stamp of religious and racial prejudice furnished the principal data to Western historians who have belittled the heroic achievements of the great Maratha king. The breezes of Maharashtra wafted a fervent inspiration over the length and breadth of the country to be breathed by many a spirited Rajput, Bundela, Jat and Sikh warrior in the Northern climes. That Shivaji rudely broke the spell of a ruthless alien tyrrany in the land was naturally bound to be an eyesore to the tyrants; but what is amazing is that some of the Western historians should have tried to perpetuate the myth of Shivaji's treachery and cruelty. Mr. C. A. Kincaid in his famous History of the Maratha People has given the lie direct to this charge in these words "Shivaji has by a curious fate suffered more at the hands of historians than any other character in history. They have one and all accepted as final the opinion of Grant Duff which again was based on that of Khafi Khan. ......And while judging Shivaji with the utmost harshness they have been singularly indulgent to his enemies. The thousand basenesses of Aurangzeb, the appalling villainies of the Bijapur and Ahmadnagar nobles have been passed over with an indulgent smile...... Shivaji however is depicted as the incarnation of successful perfidy, a Caesar Borgia......" One of the outstanding virtues of Shivaji was the unfailing

Mahomedan women and children who were taken prisoners in war. They were never forced into slavery but were honourably treated and released with a gracious indulgence. Contrast this magnanimous conduct with that of Shivaji's foes under similar circumstances. Another compelling claim to greatness of the Maratha king is the fact that he never stooped to insult the religion of his enemies; he never destroyed or desecrated mosques even under the gravest provocation or in the hour of his greatest triumph. Holy men and cultivators were invariably honourably treated by Shivaji. The Maratha soldiery practised these civilized restraints in compliance with the strict campaigning regulations laid down by their leader. Travellers from Europe who visited this country during Shivaji's lifetime have borne eloquent witness to the fact that the administration of justice in his territories was stricter and more impartial than anywhere else in India at the time.

* * * *

So sings Rabindra Nath Tagore, the illustrious muse of modern India, in his poetic and wonderfully picturesque way, which simultaneously thrills and fascinates:—

"On an obscure date in a remote century not known to me today, while you were sitting in the darkness of some forest in an unknown hill in Maharashtra, O king Shivaji, this idea came down like an electric spark illuminating your brow. 'I will knit together into one kingdom of righteousness India, which is divided, disunited and distracted.

. . . . . . . . . . . . . . . . . . . . . . . .

Then one day there came from the wide lawns of Maharashtra the flame of your thunder painting in all directions and beyond with the electric fire of numerous ages the flame of your great *Mantra.* The crown of the Mogal's helmet trembled like dry leaf on the stormy twilight of the world's end.

. . . . . . . . . . . . . . . . . . . . . . . .

Then in the depth of a storm driven night the royal palace of Delhi became empty-its festoons of lamps, one by one, from room to room, began to flicker out into darkness. . . . . . . . . . . . .

. . . . . . . . . . . . . . . . . . . . . . . .

The foreigner's history pursues you with the violent laughter of ridicule; it calls you robber. . . . . .

History, thou false science, end thy prattles. The sure writings of Providence must now triumph over thy writings. . . . . . . . . . .

O royal mendicant and Hero, your great idea has been treasured up in heaven. Can time take

What is true does never die—does never die, even beneath the forgetfulness of hundreds of centuries.

.......................................

With you today are not your standard, your legions, your martial horses, your dread weapons. Your war drums today do not sound to the cry "Hara, Hara, Hara"-maddening the sky. It is only your name that has come down today from the region of the manes, that has sent its call......

...........................

Now we have known you, known you, known you, O King.

..................................."

# Chapter VIII.

# Chhatrasal.

## Part I.

"My good blade carves the casques of men,
My tough lance thrusteth sure;
My strength is as the strength of ten,
Because my heart is pure."

*Tennyson.*

Form times immemorial the Rajput cavalier has been the soul of manly honour. He generously gives courtesy and consideration to friend and foe alike and expects the same in return. These have been the keynotes of Rajput character.

Champat Rai a scion of the royal Bundela Rajput stock had displayed great gallantry in several wars of Shah Jahan. On occassions, however, he felt slighted and ignored until the estrangement became so acute that he could no longer brook to stay at the Mogal court. His sudden departure was deeply resented by the emperor who despatched an army under general Baqi Khan to bring round the haughty Bundela chief. Easier far to tame the tiger than to cool the fiery wrath of the Rai ! Champat Rai's resources were insignificant as compared with those of the Mogal empire at the summit of its glory. Yet he swore an oath of eternal enmity to Shah Jahan. The Rajput had fully reckoned the consequences of his daring conduct which might be little short of annihilation. Some sharp engagements took place between the Mogal and Bundela forces, in which the latter were naturally worsted. Sarbahan, the 14 year old son of Champat Rai, pluckily seconded his sire in this campaign. The boy prince weilded his brand in battle with the skill of a veteran and laid low numbers among the invading host. He was bathing in a tank, one day, with a number of his playmates. The Mogal spies carried the intelligence to Baqi Khan who had Sarbahan captured and ruthlessly put to death.

Champat Rai too soon found himself a fugitive among the mountains, there to nurse the spirit of vengeance and bide his time. His noble spouse Rani Lal Kunwaree began to mourn the loss of her eldest born who had been cut down at the very threshhold of youth. But the departed hero visited his mother in a dream and assured her that he would be soon reborn to her to wreak vengeance on the foes of his race and country. The Rani felt strangely solaced by this dream. It remained no secret among the masses of the people who were inspired with the hope that a superman was coming to deliver them form the clutches of the Mogals. The dream did come true as soon after Chhatrasal was born to the Rani in 1697 A. D. in a deep cave of the wooded part of Moar hill, situated in *tehsil* Garoth of the modern Jhansi district. Inscrutable are the ways of God ! While the child is nursed in the wild hills, the cradle of independence, with no other playmates then the handful of rugged Rajput warriors who have chosen to follow the fortunes of the fearless Champat Rai, even in adversity, the shadow of a terrible tragedy creeps up to brood over Bundelkhand.

Raja Jujhar Singh of Orchha attends the Mogal court at Delhi. The state is administered during his absence by his younger brother Rajkumar Hardev Singh. The latter handles his charge so fairly and firmly as to give mortal umbrage to a wicked clique, who can no longer pilfer and fleece the people. Before long their venomous hatred leads the Raja to suspect an amour between his wife and the Rajkumar. The innocent Rani is asked to administer poison to her supposed paramour, in order to vindicate her honour. Can she refuse the ordeal ? No; and yet it means the cruel cold-blooded murder of a prince whose love for her is as pure as that of a child for its mother and vice versa. But the dark die is ruthlessly cast and she cannot forsake the peerless ideal of a Hindu wife. The Rajkumar learns of his elder brother's decision but there is not the slightest trace of resentment in his heart. On the contrary he joyfully takes the poisoned food. Some of his most devoted friends and followers hasten to the palace and partake in that grim ghoulish feast to keep company even in the Great Beyond. The fatuous Raja now begins to quake and cry. While the wails of grief and lamentation rend the sky in all directions, the saintly prince smiles serenely as if a great peace had dawned on his soul. Presently he rises and with tottering steps wends his way to the temple of Shri Raghunathji. His last moments are passed there in holy contemplation and unspoken prayer until he sinks to the floor in eternal sleep.

A thrill of indescribable horror and indignation raced through Bundelkhand like a streak of lightning. Har Dev Singhji was the idol of the people's hearts. There could be no stronger proof of the universal affection he commanded than that the populace deified the departed hero. The Raja was deeply stricken with remorse and shame but it was too late for him to regain the alienated sympathies of his subjects. They looked upon the heartless fratricide

A sense of insecurity and then turmoil swept over the luckless land. The very independence of the brave Bundelas in defence of which their ancestors had so lavishly shed their blood in the past was now jeopardised by the insensate folly of the Raja.

Shah Jahan snatched this rare opportunity to attempt the conquest of Bundelkhand. In the absence of organized resistance, the Mogal army under Khan Jahan, Khwaja Abdulla and Baqi Khan, soon overran the country and began to commit all sorts of atrocities The people had perforce to taste of the bitter cup of political servitude, until they could endure Mogal license, insults and spoliation no more. The eagle gaze of Champat Rai was keenly taking in the situation frrom his secret eyries in the hills. His patriotic soul was galled by the very idea that his native land should groan under the iron heel of the invader. His whereabouts were not unknown to the bolder spirits among his countrymen who began to flock under his banners until he considered himself strong enough to give battle to the Mogals. The Bundelas were fired by pure patriotism as much as by the fierce craving for revenge.

> "Low murmuring sounds along their banners fly;
> Revenge or death, the watchword and reply."
>
> *Campbell.*

Terrific was the clash. Baqi Khan, the murderer of Sarbahan, and Shah Baz Khan, another distinguished Mogal general, lay dead on the field of battle. The victorious Bundelas wrested Bhilsa and Dhamoni from the Mogals and burnt Sironj. In fact the whole of Bundelkhand was cleared of the foe at the end of this swift campaign. Rather than prolong the war, Shah Jahan was well advised at this stage to restore the country to a Bundela prince named Pahar Singh. This was a crafty move calculated to sow the seeds of internal discord among the Bundelas and render them an easier prey to imperial designs. What followed is a tangle of murderous intrigue aimed against the life of Champat Rai, through which however he came out unscathed.

The hour of Bundela vengeance was approaching as civil war had broken out among the sons of Shah Jahan. Aurangzeb had heard of the daring exploits of Champat Rai and wanted to win him over to his own cause. The Bundelas needed no second invitation te hasten to the aid of Murad and Aurangzeb. Dara had taken up a strong strategic position. His batteries were so planted on the northern bank of the Chambal as to command the passage of the river, so that any attempt on the part of Aurangzeb to force the crossing would have proved disastrous. Such was the anxious situation when Champat Rai, at the head of his Bundela force, joined the army of the allied brothers, to their great joy. It was the eve of the bloody battle of Shamgarh in 1658. The Rai's intimate knowledge of the country served Aurangzeb in rare stead at this critical juncture. His entire army was led to cross the Chambal at a ford near bay, which was unknown to Dara, thus completely circumventing the superior dispositions of the latter's army. On the following day the battle of Shamgarh sealed the fates of Dara and the aged Shah Jahan for ever.

Being overjoyed at this providential victory, which placed the Peacock Throne at his feet, Aurangzeb bestowed a rich *jagir* around Kalpi on Champat Rai, as a reward for his invaluable services. The Rai had captured a magnificent Arab steed in the battle of Shamgarh. As soon as Bahadur Khan, the favourite councillor of the new emperor, set his eyes on the horse he desired to possess it; but the Rai flatly refused to part with his trophy. This incident led to serious consequences as Bahadur Khan began to harbour a bitter grudge owing to his discomfiture. His intrigue soon bore its evil fruit. On Shujah's advance from Bengal, Bahadur Khan was able to arouse the emperor's displeasure against Champat Rai for alleged dilatoriness in coming to the aid of the imperial forces. What the wily Mogal courtier had counted upon came true, viz. an open rupture. The Rajput cavalier was staggered by the display of ingratitude and it served as the last momentous turning point in his romantic career. His fury took on a lurid form. He flung off his Mogal rank with the utmost contempt, sacked and burnt a part of Agra and started homewards.

Champat Rai had embarked on a regular Bhoomeawat and to the stirring strains of war drums his martial clansmen mustered strong under his banners to participate in that favourite Rajput pastime. Many a Mogal outpost was rushed and many a Mogal market was sacked by the swift striking force of the Bundela leader. Aurangzeb had soon to turn his attention to the dangerous course of affairs in Bundelkhand. He was fully aware of the internecine feuds and clannish jealousies of the Rajputs, their ancient scourge, and found little difficulty in playing off a section of the Rai's own countrymen against him. Good care was taken by Aurangzeb to back his new Bundela protege with a strong Mogal army, before he set forth with the express object of reducing Bundelkhand to the Mogal yoke. Champat Rai's heart was sad at the thought of his own degenerate kinsmen who were up in arms against him. He thus had to battle against his own kith and kin for four he was prostrated by a fearful disease. Mogal gold had found its way among Champat Rai's ranks. Eventually he was led into an ambush in 1664, while bedridden, and, rather than fall a captive into the hands of the enemy, he plunged his sword into his heart and expired. His noble consort followed suit.

## Part II.

Chhatrasal was barely 15 years of age when he was thus violently deprived of his parents' protection. His father's ceaseless war against the Mogals during the last two decades had so thoroughly inured him to privations and hardships that he remained a total stranger to luxury throughout his long life. Brought up and trained from his earliest boyhood in the school of war and adventure, Chhatrasal developed an iron frame of extraordinary physical strength and endurance. It was the early acquisition of these soldierly qualities which, coupled with a dauntless disposition and pure patriotic impulses, urged him to carve out an independent kingdom for himself in defiance of the incomparably superior might of a monarch like Aurangzeb.

The heart of the spirited boy was brimming with bitterness at the base treachery which had convassed elder brother Angad Rai, a great warrior, and the two resolved to quit their native land to seek their fortunes in the wider world beyond. It so happened that Maharajah Siwai Jai Singh was, at the time, passing through Bundelkhand on his way back from the Deccan. The two brothers went to see him and obtained honourable rank in the Mogal army. They were attached to an imperial force under Nawab Bahadur Khan who had been deputed to punish the rebel governor of Devgarh. With the young Rajput blood coursing hotly through his veins, Chhatrasal was delighted with the expedition, as it held out chances of winning distinction just as his father had won at the battle of Shamgarh. But the Rajput boy was not yet initiated into the tortuous ways of court preferment. The headlong valour of Chhatrasal materially contributed to the victory of the imperial force at Devgarh. He was badly wounded and being missed, his clansmen searched the field of battle far and wide; but in vain. On the following morning, a trooper informed them that a fine horse was keeping guard over a fallen soldier at some distance towards the east of the battlefield. He and his friends had tried to seize the horse but the faithful animal would not let anybody approach near its master. The hopes of Chhatrasal's retainers revived on hearing this strange narrative.

They hurried to the spot and were rewarded by the sight of their prince, who lay unconscious in a pool of blood. He was brought to the camp and was cured in due course.

The selfish Nawab, though profuse in verbal praises of the heroic conduct of Chhatrasal, had never mentioned a word about it in his official despatches, which attributed the victory entirely to his own martial prowess. Accordingly the emperor granted him an increase in rank but Chhatrasal failed to get the slightest recognition of his sterling services. This produced such a tremendous revulsion of feelings in the heart of the young Rajput as to change the entire course of his life and simultaneously the history of Bundelkhand. Not unoften have trifling incidents like this changed the destinies of men and nations. Chhatrasal, though still quite immature in age and experience, was set furiously thinking. The emperor's religious persecutions, ingratitude and selfishness all rushed back in vivid recollection to his susceptible mind. His father had gallantly stood forth as the champion of independence; then why could not he? What bond in common had he with the arrogant Mogals? On the contrary he remembered he had heavy scores to settle against them. These volcanic ideas and intentions were richly nourished by the shining precept of Shivaji whose daring exploits were then the theme of universal admiration in the country. The sudden shock of ingratitude had destroyed the young prince's faith in the Mogals and aroused secret yearnings which struggled for decisive expression and direction.

Before Chhatrasal had decided on any particular course of action against the Mogals, his force received orders to proceed to the Deccan in order to join the army operating against Shivaji. Chhatrasal was secretly overjoyed at this news and formed his resolution instantaneously. The winter of 1670 had now set in. With a few companions, he left the Mogal camp one day, to hunt in the jungle, but the real objective was the fort of Raigarh. For years he had cherished the longing to see the great Maratha patriot Shivaji, and confer with him. The handful of adventurous Rajputs boldly struck out westwards even without a guide. They hunted the boar and deer for food by day, while some knowledge of the stars at night helped them on towards their destination. At last the river Krishna was crossed on an improvised raft and they stepped on Maratha territory. Fortunately for them Shivaji happened to be present in the vicinity. The national bard tenderly dwells on every detail of the historic meeting beween the two famous warriors, the one

Chhatrasal

of age, having already achieved success in his exalted mission of life; the other, an inexperienced youth, yet at the foot of the ladder of life though pulsating with the same lofty ambitions and ideals as his elderly companion. Shivaji clasped the Bundela youth to his bosom and urged him to follow in the noble wake of his father. "Put your trust in God and strike hard for the independence of Bundelkhand. Drive out the Mogals and never put faith in their pledges. Our aims and interests are identical". Such was briefly the soul stirring counsel of the great hero of the Deccan. Needless to say that every word of it found a corresponding echo in the heart of Chhatrasal. On departure Shivaji invested him with a fine sword of honour. And what more appropriate gift there could be from one soldier of freedom to another ?

Chhatrasal unfurled the flag of independence on his return to Bundelkhand. The news spread like wildfire through the country and large numbers of his bolder comrades and kinsmen flocked to serve under him. The calculating sceptics however held back in the belief that the revolt of the hot-blooded youth would be sternly quelled by Aurangzeb. It so happened that the emperor sent Fidai Khan at this time with orders to the governor of Gwalior to raze the Hindu temples of Orchha to the ground and to promulgate the Mahomedan law. Accordingly a Mogal army under Fidai Khan himself entered Bundelkhand to execute these orders. Chhatrasal was furious on receipt of this intelligence and one of his trusty Sardars, named Dhurmangad, attacked the Mogal with such determination as to throw them into headlong flight. This success had an important sequal as it gained to Chhatrasal such an important ally as Raja Sujan Singh of Orchha who plucked up courage and cast in his lot with the fortunes of the young patriot. When the two Rajput leaders met, they placed a naked sword between them and swore eternal friendship through thick and thin.

Chhatrasal learnt that Prabhu Pran Nath, the celebrated religious teacher from Kathiawar, had come to Mahewa and forthwith proceeded to pay his respects to him. This Mahatma was one of those several saints who moved from place to place during the dark days of Aurangzeb's religious persecutions, exhorting the Hindus to hold fast to their religion and to organize. Something in Chhatrasal's martial bearing and the steady fire of his eyes kindled the interest of the Mahatma to such a degree that he took him to Panna and revealed the existence of the diamond mines to him. Now, imagine a scene at Panna. In the romantic valley of the hill of Mandartung, the sage Pran Nath seats Chhatrasal on a slab of rock, near a bank of the Dharmasagar Tank, and annoints his forehead with the holy *tilak*. A brief prayer in clear crisp tones follows to invoke divine guidance and help in the cause of Bundela independence. The sage rises and girds his own sword round the loins of Chhatrasal as an omen of victory. And a mighty roar of "Victory to Chhatrasal" issues from thousands of manly throats.

Chhatrasal soon accummulated a considerable treasure by the sale of the diamonds excavated at Panna, which enabled him to launch his preparations for war an a larger scale than was otherwise possible. The fact that he had taken the celebrated Prabhu Pran Nath as his spiritual guide and preceptor, and been blessed by him, flung out an irresistible appeal to the heart of Bundelkhand. Victory, treasure and reputation, after all, proved to be links in the evolution of Chhatrasal's destiny. His noble resolutions and buoyant spirits attracted the brave Bundelas to him like a magnet from far and near. The people remembered the historic dream of his mother and began to identify in him the promised deliverer. Not that Chhatrasal relied altogether on popular credulity; he was a man of action out and out. His ubiquitous messengers were out to inspire and organize the people in every nook and corner.

of Bundelkhand. Chhatrasal soon began to gather the fruits of his dynamic activity. The leading Sardars of the country including Kanwar Narain Das, Govind Rai Pramar, Sundar Mani, Megh Raj Parihar, and Kishori Singh assembled under his banners to partake in the war of independence. Day by day the movement gathered weight and momentum by the arrival of fresh levies.

Chhatrasal made his preparations so silently and swiftly that the Mogals barely found cause for much alarm. To start with, he decided to wreak his vengeance on the traitors who had played false to his father. Their village was sacked and their castle was razed to the ground. This exploit served to open the eyes of the Mogals. Mahomed Hashim, the governor of Sironj, sent a force of Pathans to oppose Chhatrasal but they were routed without difficulty and fled back into Sironj. The news caused serious uneasiness among the neighbouring military stations of the Mogals. The governor of Dhamoni, Khaliq Khan, took the field in person. He was defeated wherever he made a stand until he was adroitly surrounded by Chhatrasal and the entire Mogal camp, kettle drums, camels and horses were seized as loot of war. Khaliq Khan was forced to yeild a cash indemnity of Rs. 30,000/- before his life was spared. Chhatrasal followed up this success by a swift attack on Maihar and captured the town. He next attacked Basa and slew its chief in single combat.

Actuated by a policy of ceaseless offensive, which suited the temper of his young army to a nicety, Chhatrasal began to commit sudden irruptions into the territories of the neighbouring Mahomedan chiefs. He defeated Sayyad Bahadur and Sayyad Munawwar in such rapid succession that the whole country around Gwalior lay at his feet and was leisurely plundered by the Bundelas. Chhatrasal now turned south and by forced marches suddenly presented himself before the fort of Garhkot in Saugor district. The Mogals were caught napping and were forced to capitulate. Mahomed Hashim made a final attempt to oppose Chhatrasal but was hopelessly defeated. The latter began to levy regular *Chowth* in the conquered territories after the Maratha fashion, which enormously augmented his limited resources. But a rich collateral advantage of this sharp succession of victories was that some of the leading Sardars like Ratan Shah, Sabal Shah, Amar Diwan, Prithiraj, Madho Rai and Parbat Singh, who had so far been watching from the fence, came over to join the national war. In a word, no less than 70 princes of royal Bundela blood, with all their retainers and dependents, had now collected under the banners of Chhatrasal, which marked the fruition of his herculean efforts to mobilise the manhood of Bundelkhand.

> "Beneath each banner proud to stand,
> Looked up the noblest of the land."
>
> *Scott.*

This unexpected mobilisation, in 1680, so frightened Khaliq Khan that he appealed to Aurangzeb for immediate reinforcements, in order to stem the tide of Bundela aggression. Accordingly the emperor despatched a large army under Ran Dulah Khan, one of the best known generals of his time, with 22 other grandees of rank. Passing through Datia and Orchha, it arrived at Garhkot where Chhatrsal lay encamped to await the Mogal onset. He had never before fought such an overwhelming and well equipped imperial army in the open field. But the heart of the Bundela hero became steeled as the hour of action drew near. The battle began in the morning and raged with unabated fury throughout the day without any side claiming advantage. Thousands lay dead on the field of battle which was carried on in the dark after sunset. At midnight Chhatrasal broke through one of the Mogal wings by an irresistible cavalry charge and threw them into hopeless confusion. The gunners were outflanked and cut down at their posts, when the remnants of the erstwhile proud Mogal army fled from the field.

Aurangzeb was furious with Ran Dulah Khan on receipt of this sorry intelligence and despatched another army under general Baqa Khan Rumi to crush the Bundelas. Chhatrasal gave battle to this host at Bassia and gained a decisive victory again. He followed up this success so resolutely as to overrun the districts of Banda and Hamirpur, and marching through Saugor he surprised the Mogals in Narwar and gave up the district to the fire and the sword. The emperor was severely shocked on receipt of the news of the second defeat. He was directing operations from Ajmer in the war against Marwar and his mind was already a prey to numerous anxieties and worries owing to the recent desertion of Prince Akbar who had gone over to the Rathores. It was fortunate for the Bundelas that during the last quarter of the 17th century the armies of the Mogal empire were being drained in two large theatres of war, viz. the Deccan and Rajasthan. Seething discontent within the empire, which necessitated the maintenance of armed garrisons all over the country, and ceaseless war at several outposts had strained the military resources of Aurangzeb to such a degree that he could not concentrate on the subjugation of Bundelkhand.

At the close of 1680 Aurangzeb deputed his famous general Tahawwur Khan to check the growing depredations of Chhatrasal. The approach of the Mogal army synchronised with the dates of Chhatrasal's marriage. He had already received intelligence of the Mogals' plans and gave such a hot reception to his assailants that Tahawwur Khan beat a precipitate retreat from the field. The marriage ceremonies were thus not interrupted and Chhatrasal departed with his noble bride, plundering Dhamoni and the Kalanjar district on his way. Tahawwur Khan could endure these insults no longer and came on in full strength to try conclusions with the Bundelas. A sanguinary battle ensued in which several leading chiefs of both sides were killed. About sunset the Mogal line began to waver. Chhatrasal who was closely observing the development of the new phase in the battle ordered a general assault. It resulted in a debacle among ths Mogals, as expected.

These substantial victories went far to enhance the martial renown of Chhatrasal. In 1687 he formally installed himself as independent Maharajah of the conquered territories. He seized several other towns from the Mogals. Nibholi was burnt down and Jalalpur was sacked. A force under Sayyad Latif which had dared to attack the

Bundelas was so roughly handled that it had to fly leaving behind all its camp equipage, horses and elephants. The neighbouring Mogal *subedars* were at this time on the tenterhooks of perpetual anxiety as it was never known where the next Bundela blow would fall. In fact Chhatrasal was carrying on war and plunder in Mogal territories with a vengeance. Numbers of towns on the Mogal border were surprised, their officers seized and treasure looted. Mahoba was sacked. Chhatrasal's lightning raids extended as far as Bhilsa., Ujjain and Garh Chanda and the whole country thus overrun was forced to yeild *Chowth.*

Aurangzeb could not afford to look on with indifference. He sent an army under the command of Sheikh Mahomed Anwar to wrest back the Mogal districts from the Bundelas. The Sheikh met with no better fate than his predecessors. The Mogal army was routed and the Sheikh was captured alive, with all his artillery and war stores. He was obliged to purchase his personal safety by paying a cash amount of Rs. 2 lakhs to his Rajput victor.

On receipt of the news of this serious disaster, a special Darbar was convened at Delhi to cope with the menace. After due deliberations a fresh army under Mirza Sadruddin Irani, a tried general, was ordered to invade Bundelkhand. Chhatrasal took up a strategic position in the jungle near Panna, where a desperate battle ensued. Luck shone on his banners once more and the vainglorious Mirza sought his safety in flight. After this, the opposition of smaller Mogal chiefs like Hamid Khan and Latif Khan was easily overcome. In fact the latter was taken prisoner and was made to pay an indemnity of Rs. 1 lakh.

The orbit of Chhatrasal's devastating activities in Mogal territory was expanding. He ventured to penetrate it so far as he could preserve the safety of his line of communications with the home bases. The mind of the aging emperor was racked by impotent rage, and unmitigated alarm. He made a last despairing effort to recover his lost supremacy over Bundelkhand. The country was invaded by a powerful army under Abdul Samad Khan Turani, who came to grips with the Bundelas in the forests near Panna. A battle of singular ferocity was fought. Fortune favoured the brave Bundelas. The Turani warrior-nobleman was outclassed in military strategy by his Rajput antagonist. At sunset Abdul Samad Khan applied for a truce to enable him to bury the heaps of dead Mogals. Next morning he paid the inevitable *Chowth* and was allowed to depart unmolested. Chhatrasal marched into Panna amidst the song of victory and welcome.

Guj Singh a distinguished chief of the Bundela army surprised Bhilsa and sacked and burnt the town. This daring raid so enraged the governor, Behlol Khan, that he took the field with 9000 mail clad troops and 300 guns. He attacked Damoh, then a part of Chhatrasal's territories, which was known to be empty of Bundela forces. Kunwar Jagat Singh, a son of Chhatrasal's brother, who happened to be present in the neighbourhood gallantly struck in to save the town from disaster. A continuous battle of seven days and nights followed, which may be justly reckoned as the Thermopylae of Bundelkhand. Needless to say that the self sacrifice of this small Bundela band averted the otherwise fearful fate of Damoh. Time was gained to rush up reinforcements. Full of rage at being thus baulked of his prey, Behlol marched on Rajgarh and besieged the fort. It was strongly garrisoned and well stocked. The Bundelas struck terror among the Mogals by their brilliant sorties. One day Behlol Khan was badly wounded while riding an elephant, which so dispirited him that he raised the siege and returned to Dhamoni, only to die.

Chhatrasal invaded the environs of Mahoba again and plundered the country until he was opposed by Murad Khan, the chief of Singhura, who refused to pay *Chowth*. The Pathans fought bravely but one thousand of them, including Murad Khan, were slain. Their camp, standards, Toshakhana and 1400 horses fell into the hands of the Bundelas who then sacked Singhura at leisure. Chhatrasal now wheeled round and overran the whole extent of country from Konch to Mhow realising *Chowth* at the point of the sword. Said Afgan Khan, Shah Quli Khan and other Mogal grandees who endeavoured to withstand the Bundela avalanche were in turn badly beaten and forced to pay heavy indemnities. In short by the close of the 17th century, Chhatrasal had consolidated his conquests in Central India so securely that the Mogals had little inclination left to attack such a redoubtable champion, who had already inflicted a series of humiliating defeats on some of the most famous generals of the Mogal empire. Moreover Aurangzeb was dying and with him the hectic glory of the empire was fast fading into the shadows of speedy dissolution.

The new emperor Bahadur Shah maintained friendly relations with Chhatrasal throughout his brief reign of 5 years. On the death of the former in 1712, the empire was plunged into the throes of a murderous internecine war of succession. Farrukh Sayyar, who ascended the throne, in 1713, with the help of the Sayyad brothers, was little better than a puppet in their hands. He was persuaded to grant a *Sanad* to Nawab Mahomed Khan Bangash of Farrukhabad for the possession of certain territories of Chhatrasal. Accordingly the Nawab attacked Chhatrasal but met with no success. Jagat Rai, the second son of Chhatrasal, defeated the Nawab in pitched battle and killed Diler Khan a prominent Mogal chief. The Nawab retreated and gave up his projected offensive against Bundelkhand. As a matter of fact the Mogal empire was fast crumbling to peices. The court was a hotbed of intrigue and total anarchy prevailed in all the distant provinces.

Peace reigned over Chhatrasal's dominions for over another decade. In 1725 Bangash invaded Bundelkhand again to settle old scores. After six months of continuous war, in which none of the combatants gained much advantage, the Nawab received orders to hasten to Malwa, which had been invaded by the Marathas under Bajee Rao. The departure of the Nawab was a signal for the Bundelas to ravage the Mogal territories in all directions. Chhatrasal now forced such widely distant places as Allahabad and Mirzapur in the north and Raipur in the Deccan to yeild *Chowth.* On 4th January 1727 he re-entered Bundelkhand. The Nawab followed soon after, the Marathas having left for the Deccan, and launched a vigorous offensive against the Bundelas.

As the war was protracted for several years and the aged Chhatrasal felt that he could not carry it on successfully single-handed, he decided after consultation with his ministers, to solicit the aid of Bajee Rao. This invitation chimed in splendidly with the Peishwa's vigorous endeavours for uprooting the Mogal Empire in Hindustan. Bajee Rao was only too glad to grasp this opportunity. He set forth for Central India again in 1731 and after some sharp encounters easily drove out the Mogals from Bundelkhand.

There were rejoicings all over and the formidable Maratha champion was justly hailed as the deliverer of Bundelkhand. Chhatrasal evinced his roayl gratitude by adopting Bajee Rao as his godson and equally distributed his vast territories in Central India-comprising all the present Bundela States, portions of Gwalior and Tonk States, Saugor, Jhansi and Hamirpur districts-between his legitimate sons Hirday Shah and Jagat Rai and his son by adoption, Bajee Rao. Two years after the close of the war, Chhatrasal passed away to eternal rest. A cenotaph stands in his memory in the village of Mow in Chhatarpur State.

# Chapter IX.

# Guru Govind Singh.

"The fearful sufferings of the land
Inflamed his heart and nerved his hand."

Jahangir, the pleasure-loving emperor, could hardly have dreamt that the incarceration of Guru Arjun, in 1606, would sow the seeds of that bitter hate which was destined to consume the power of the later Mogals in the Land of the Five Rivers. The Guru was tortured and died in his confinement near Lahore. This cruel treatment of the 5th Sikh Apostle, who bore the gentle torch of Nanak, tore the hearts of his followers with impotent rage. The Hindus of the Punjab, at this time, were virtually a fallen race whose political ambitions had been crushed long ago by centuries of subjection under the bigoted Mahomedan rulers of the land. As a matter of fact the warrior caste among the Hindus had been driven from the alluvial plains of the Punjab by the fury of the early Mahomedan invasions. Those who remained trod the peaceful paths of industry and agriculture on sufferance at the hands of their political masters. They had to bow low before the waves of bigotry, oppression and wrong which passed over their heads every now aud then. Disintegerated by the wooden walls of caste, the Hindus' pursuit of religion had degenerated into an unreasoning and lifeless ritual, which furnished them little inspiration to emancipate themselves from the closely woven meshes of political servitude.

Guru Nanak was a venerable pioneer of reform in Hindu society. His successors developed and systematized the new faith, distinguished as much by the grandeur of its simplicity as by its intense fervour of popular appeal. Some years after the martyrdom of Guru Arjun, Jahangir ordered his son and successor, Guru Har Govind, to be confined in the fort of Gwalior, where he passed twelve long years in dreary captivity in a state of semi-starvation. Handsome and warlike of disposition, Guru Har Govind initiated a military policy among his followers, after his return from Gwalior. He armed them and adopted a baronial character. His forces frequently came into conflict with Mogal troops, sent by the governor of Lahore to suppress them, and gained several successes. The rank ignorance and misery of the masses in the Punjab, rendered them peculiarly open to suggestion. Before long the Sikhs developed into a military brotherhood closely knit together by the ties of a common faith. Their human passions were inflamed by the harsh religious persecution to which they were subjected by the Mogal government. Guru Har Govind was the first to introduce meat diet among his disciples so as to make them better fitted for the pursuit of war. He enjoined upon them to observe strict religious equality among themselves. In short the political genius and warlike propensities of the Guru produced a wonderful effect in toning down the sturdy Sikhs into hard fighting stuff. During the reign of the two succeeding Gurus the evolution of Sikh society steadily progressed.

Guru Har Kishan, the 8th Apostle, having died in 1664, he was succeeded by Guru Tegh Bahadur. While the latter was away towards Bengal with his wife Gujri, Govind Singh was born to them at Patna in the year 1660. On his return to the Punjab, Guru Tegh Bahadur took to a predatory career and plundered a large tract of fertile country along the banks of the Sutlej. By this time the fanatical policy of Aurangzeb, the reigning Mogal emperor, was in full swing. Hindu temples were being destroyed: Hindus were being driven out of the offices of state; numerous handicaps were placed on the free exercise of their religion and every humiliation was being heaped on their heads. The emperor did not even stop short at force, open or veiled, to convert the unbelievers to Islam. The Sikhs naturally came in for their full share of his rancorous attentions not only for professing the Sikh faith but also on account of the depredations caused by their Guru in the Sutlej valley. Many a Sikh was executed and many more were tortured and brutally treated in other ways. The heart of Guru Tegh Bahadur was sore with the endless tale of forcible conversions and atrocities which reached his ears from all parts of the country.

One day a band of learned Brahmins from Kashmere approached the Guru with their tale of woe and entreated him to devise some means to safeguard the Hindu religion. For a moment the Guru was plunged in thought and then replied "The crisis demands that some Mahatma should sacrifice himself at the altar of religion." At this young Govind Singh, the Guru's son, reverently stood forth and addressing his father exclaimed "Who can be a greater Mahatma than yourself !" Guru Tegh Bahadur was thrilled to the core by his son's logic, radiant with the loftiest ideal of human duty and forthwith conveyed a message to Aurangzeb to try to convert him to Islam instead of terrorizing the masses who would surely follow in the Guru's wake. The emperor approved of the suggestion and the Guru, with five of his chosen disciples, was ordered to repair to Delhi. He realised full well that he was going to court martyrdom. Before he set out for the capital, the Guru sent for his son, the gallant Govind Singh, and girding on his loins the sword of Guru Har Govind, enjoined upon him to wreak vengeance on the foes of their race and religion. When Guru Tegh Bahadur and his companions reached Delhi, in 1675, Aurangzeb sent several Qazis to persuade them to embrace Islam. But the Sikh heroes were unshakeable in their religious beliefs. The Qazis went back discomfited and shamefaced. The emperor was enraged and ordered the prisoners to be put to death. A steel saw was worked on the head of Bhai Mani Das to saw him into two parts; Bhai Dayala was thrown alive into a cauldron of boiling oil; Guru Tegh Bahadur was beheaded and his remaining companions were simultaneously done to death with similar barbarous cruelties.

> "Their country conquers with their martyrdom,
> And Freedom's fame finds wings on every wind."
>
> *Byron.*

Those savage atrocities lashed the Sikh people into fury and sowed the seeds of undying hate in their hearts against their oppressors. The Sikhs had not forgotten how Guru Arjun had been similarly martyred and the cruel incarceration of Guru Har Govind not very long ago. They had by now completely come under the influence of a mass-psychosis. For the time, their armed strength was practically dissipated by the harsh severities of Aurangzeb and his iconoclastic lieutenants in the Punjab. Guru Govind Singh was now just in the middle of his teens. Though burning to avenge the violent murder of his father and the numerous wrongs inflicted on his race, he had yet to take stock of his bearings and act with the utmost caution. He was surrounded by numerous foes, including some of his nearest kinsmen, who had banded together to oppose his accession to the holy *gaddee*. Like all truly great men, however, the young Guru was not at all dismayed by the overwhelming forces arrayed against him. He decided to retire into some place of safety in the hills where he could calmly deliberate, mature his plans and form a rallying centre for his followers. There he nursed the spirit of revenge in his quiet retreat in the Siwaliks and made the glorious resolve to liberate his race from its political bondage. The early manhood of Guru Govind Singh was thus passed in seclusion.

This period may be reckoned as the time of careful preparation for the accomplishment of his vast designs in the future. He assiduously devoted himself to religious and historical studies acquiring thereby a rich store of knowledge. For this purpose he had secured the services of several Pandits who taught him Hindi and Sanscrit and initiated him into the sacred lore of the Shastras; and Maulvis who taught him Persian and court etiquette. The thrilling tales of the Mahabharat, Ramayana and Puranas left a permanent impression on the mind of the youthful Guru. In his later life he never forgot how Rama had taken birth to destroy Ravan and Krishna to destroy the monstrous Kans. In fact the Guru devoutly believed that whenever *Dharma* is jeopardised by the iniquities of a tyrant, God the Almighty appears in human form, as an incarnation, to destroy the tyrant and save *Dharma*. This belief has been beautifully expressed in *Vichitra Natak*, the famous poem composed by Guru Govind Singh. Not content with his own acquisition of learning, the Guru was anxious to raise the intellectual level of his followers and to secure this end he employed about 50 Brahmins to translate the important Hindu scriptures into the popular language. He despatched five young Sikhs to Benares to acquire deeper learning and on their return to the Punjab after the completion of their studies, the Guru selected another batch of five and sent them off to Benares for the same object. This remarkable effort was maintained for a number of years with excellent results.

In 1684, Raja Medni Prakash of Nahan sent an affectionate invitation to Guru Govind Singh to visit his capital. This being accepted, the Guru was welcomed at Nahan with great honour. The friendship between the Raja and his guest soon ripened. The former used to listen to the Guru's religious discourses with faith and unbounded esteem. They used to go together to hunt big game in the hills and forests of the Raja's dominions. One day the Guru sent for Raja Fateh Chand of Srinagar, who bore a deep grudge against the Raja of Nahan and brought about a complete reconciliation between them. During the same year Guru Govind Singh built a fort at Paonta, as advised by the Raja of Nahan, another at Chamkaur, near Ropar, and a third one at Anandpur. The Guru had become an expert in the use of arms and horsemanship. He fervently believed that his exalted mission in life was to regenerate his fallen race and to destroy the tyrrany of the Mogal government.

> "He had left his home in his spirit's pride,
> With his father's sword and blessing;
> He stood with the valiant side by side,
> His country's wrongs redressing."

*L. E. Lunding.*

Guru Govind Singh

Before embarking on an aggressive policy Guru Govind Singh decided to propitiate Durga, the goddess of War, not only to secure an omen but to hearten his own followers. Pandit Kesho Das, a renowned Brahmin scholar of Benares, was chosen to perform the arduous ceremonies in connection with the *yagya.* An expenditure of rupees two lakhs was sanctioned by the Guru to provide the incense which was continuously burnt for several months in a huge sacrificial pit on the summit of Naina Devi, a hill situated at a distance of ten miles from Makhowal. To conform with the austere rites as enjoined by the Shastras, the Guru observed *brahmcharya,* ate little and spoke little until the ceremonies were completed. At last the terrible goddess, enveloped in raging elements, appeared before her awestruck worshipper, who presented his sword on which the gratified deity is said to have left a mark and then disappeared. The Guru's fame spread far and wide over the Land of the Five Rivers at this miracle. And people came to believe in him as the chosen scourge of God to put down tyrrany and wrong.

Having realised that the rigours of caste and the blind bigotry of the Hindu masses, with all the attendant social wrong and disintegeration, were genuine obstacles in the path of their political salvation, Guru Govind Singh determined to remodel the faith. He swept aside all distinctions of caste by taking in converts from every class irrespective of race or descent. He directed every Sikh to call himself a Singh, meaning lion. Prior to this only the Kshattriyas, i. e. the warrior caste, used to bear the surname of Singh. With rare foresight the Guru thus raised his own followers to the level of Kshattriyas; in other words he instituted a fresh order of true Kshattriyas who were sworn to fight injustice and put down wrong. Drunk with the nectar of the Guru's spirited teachings, which broke down all artificial barriers between man and man, the Sikhs began to aspire to the highest pinnacles of earthly power. The breath of democracy and martial enthusiasm ennobled the outlook of the meanest among them. Guru Govind Singh ordered every Sikh family, possessing adult males, to furnish its quota of recruits for military service. Thus an army of 8000 men was soon mobilised at Makhowal. Already the warlike proclivities of the Guru had come to be known all over the country and this fact induced his followers to present him with horses, arms and accoutrements of war in ever larger numbers. To enhance the military efficiency of the Sikhs, Guru Govind Singh enjoined upon them the necessity of wearing the five K's, as they are called, viz. *kirpan, kesh, katch, kara* and *kangha.* He gave his disciples the name of Khalsa, or the chosen people. He proclaimed himself to be the last of the Gurus in whom individually the spirit of Guru Nanak would reside for the last time; after him it would be present in the midst of every gathering of five or more Sikhs. For a period of twenty years Guru Govind Singh thus strenuously worked in the seclusion of the hills to organize his followers on a military basis and infuse his own fiery spirit among them.

Some of the hill Rajas who were jealous of the Guru's rising power wanted to stand in the way of his political designs. As they scornfully held aloof inspite of his eloquent appeals to cooperate with him in the war of independence, he permitted the war bands of the Khalsa to ravage the territories of the hostile Rajas. Labouring under a sense of humiliation the Rajas of Nalagarh, Bilaspur and Katocha with their auxiliaries formed a strong coalition in 1686 and attacked Guru Govind Singh with an army of ten thousand men near the village of Bhangni. Unfortunately a force of 500 Pathans, whom the Guru had engaged in his service at the instance of his friend Sayyad Buddhe Shah of Sadhaura, was bribed by the Rajas to desert him. As soon as the gallant Sayyad learnt of this defection he hurried to assist his friend with a fresh force of 2000 soldiers. This timely succour turned the tide of battle, although the issue had hung in doubt in its earlier stages. Guru Govind Singh slew Raja Hari Chand of Nalagarh with his own hand and inflicted a crushing defeat on the army of the allies. He proceeded to Paonta after this victory and held a formal Darbar in which presents and robes of honour were bestowed on all those who had rendered distinguished services in the recent battle.

The Guru now built a number of new forts—Lohgarh, Anandgarh, Phulgarh and Fatehgarh—to strengthen his position. As a matter of fact he was pooling his still limited resources and developing them to wage war on the Mogals, which was the guiding spirit of his manifold activities. But were his people in a mood to make the enormous sacrifices which a war with the all powerful government would require ? That was the question with agitated the mind of the Guru day after day. In order to tap the real feelings of the Sikhs, he convened a public *Darbar* on a hillock, named Kesar Garh, near the village of Anandpur. After the people had assembled, Guru Govind Singh suddenly emerged from his tent, brandishing a naked sword and demanded a volunteer who would offer his head for sacrifice at the altar of national independence. This solemn utterance and the sword, gleaming in the bright sunlight, presented a terrible proposal to the audience. Bhai Daya Singh, a Khatri, was the first to spring up and offer his head for the proposed sacrifice. The Guru led the bold volunteer inside his tent; the thud of a stroke was heard and blood streamed out of the tent. Presently the Guru reappeared with his reeking sword and blood-splashed clothes; he asked for a second volunteer. The audience was awe-stricken. Some of the cowards had slunk away but the large majority of the Sikhs manfully held their ground. In response to the Guru's second call, Dharam Singh-a Jat from Hastinapur-boldly rose in his seat and was as before led into the Guru's tent. A fresh stream of blood gushed out of the tent, following the sound of a second stroke. In this manner the Guru led five men in succession into his tent. He had seen that the Sikhs wavered no more; nor flinched from the frightful ordeal. Then to the dazed surprise of the onlookers he brought these five men from his tent back among their comrades; the blood that had flowed was of five goats which had been previously tied within the tent for the purpose. The inflexible courage of that Sikh gathering brought to the quick intelligence of their politic leader an augury of success in his noble venture. These volunteers, named the *Panj Piyare*, or the five dear disciples of the Guru, were then helped to prepare a sweet dish out of which the whole audience including the great Guru partook. His master mind had not only judged the temper of the people, but it had also stamped a lasting impression on their minds and cemented them into a union of equal comradeship.

Guru Govind Singh formally declared war on the Mogals in 1695. Luckily the time was opportune for this daring enterprise, as Aurangzeb was battling in far away Deccan with all his might and main in the vain endeavour to overcome the hydra-headed Maratha resistance. The emissaries of the Guru succeeded in persuading Raja Bhim Chand of Kahlur to shake off the Mogal yoke. Accordingly the Raja refused to pay the annual tribute into the imperial treasury and openly allied himself with the Khalsa. This example served as a beacon light to the other hill chiefs who followed suit. For several years this state of affairs continued unchecked, until Aurangzeb was constrained to despatch an army under Jahan Khan, Zulfiqar Khan and Alif Khan to compel the defaulting Rajas to pay up their arrears of tribute by force of arms. Guru Govind Singh hastened to the aid of his allies with the consequence that the imperia army was completely defeated at Nadaun by the combined Hindu and Khalsa forces. The Guru seized the opportunity to overrun a large stretch of Mogal territory up to Ropar on the left bank of the Sutlej.

As the insurrection was assuming dangerous proportions Dilawar Khan, the governor of Kangra, received peremptory orders from the court to cope with the situation. He took the field in person against the hill Rajas and sent off his son, Rustam Khan, to attack the Guru in Anandpur, thereby driving a strong wedge between the forces of his enemies. While Rustam Khan lay encamped near the Guru's stronghold, there was such a heavy downpour of rain one night that his camp was carried away by the torrent and large numbers of his soldiers were drowned. The consternation caused by this unlooked for disaster obliged Rustam Khan to beat a precipitate retreat from the neighbourhood. Aurangzeb was greatly exasperated on receipt of this sorry intelligence and appointed his son Moazzam to command the operations in the Punjab. As Nand Lal, the secretary of the prince, was an admirer of the Guru, he prevailed upon Moazzam to put down the revolt in the hills rather than attempt to pursue a religious leader, who was of secondary political importance. The prince and his principal lieutenant, Mirza Beg, accordingly directed all their energies to subdue the Rajas. Mirza Beg forced his way into the interior of the hills and began to give up village after village to the flames. Hundreds of prisoners were caught, whose faces were blackened, and were then paraded on donkeys to strike terror in the country. Unable to withstand the imperial forces, the hill chiefs at last laid down their arms and made peace with the emperor.

Guru Govind Singh was very angry at their submission and, as the Rajas refused to help him any more, took up an aggressive attitude towards them. The Sikhs entered the territories of these Rajas near the foot of the Siwalik hills and committed a series of depredations which caused widespread alarm among them. A growing and hostile power close to them spelt political danger. Impelled by their fears the Rajas sent repeated complaints of Sikh excesses to the emperor and urged on him the need to extirpate the Guru who dared to call himself the *Sacha Badshah*, or the True King. Aurangzeb ordered the governors of Lahore and Sirhind to effectually crush the uprising of the Sikhs. Accordingly in 1701, a Mogal army under Nahar Khan and Khwaja Mahomed marched against Guru Govind Singh who faced them at Kirtipur. The proud Mogal generals sent a messenger to the Guru to warn him that he was not now pitched against petty hill chiefs but against the irresistible army of the emperor of India and that the wisest course open to him was to embrace Islam and seek for imperial pardon. Ajit Sing, a son of the Guru, was so much enraged at this arrogant speech that he drew his sword and threatened to decapitate the Mogal messenger if he would utter another word derogatory to the honour of the Guru. Back went the Mogal, crestfallen and venomous in mood. The Mogals now pressed the attack and after desperate resistance Guru Govind Singh was obliged by sheer weight of numbers to fall back on Anandpur. But the place was soon besieged by the Mogals. Gujri, mother of the Guru, along with his two sons Zorawar Singh and Fateh Singh, effected their escape from here to Sirhind.

The refugees were however captured and produced before Wazir Khan, the governor of the province. He was much impressed by the handsome and dignified bearing of the two boys and decided to keep them as hostages at his court. One day Wazir Khan playfully spoke to them. "Boys ! what would you do if I were to set you free ?" "We would fight you at the head of our followers and try to kill you" promptly replied the boys. "But what if you were defeated ?" asked the governor. Nothing daunted the boys again replied "In that case we will collect our Sikhs and again fight you to the death."

"We're the sons of sires that baffled
Crowned and mitred tyrrany:
They defied the field and scaffold
For their birthrights-so will we."

*Campbell.*

The governor was taken aback and completely upset at these uncompromising replies-cool and sharp as truest steel. He consulted the *Ulema* who passed the sentence of death on the lads but gave them a last chance of life if they embraced Islam. How could the idea of turning apostates appeal to the brave offspring of the lion-hearted leader of the Khalsa ? Needless to say that the offer was rejected with haughty disdain. The boy heroes were then walled alive. Their grandmother Gujri died of grief at their untimely end.

Meanwhile Guru Govind Singh was being hard pressed in the fort of Makhowal by the besieging Mogals. At last the scanty garrison ran short of provisions and were reduced to severe straits. When about forty adherents only were left with the Guru, it was resolved to quit the fort rather than court inevitable destruction within. One night the whole party silently slipped out of the fort, eluded the vigilance of the Mogal sentinels, and headed for the fort of Chamkaur. Their escape was however soon discovered by the Mogals, who came rushing in hot pursuit after them. A fierce engagement took place in the vicinity of the fort. Ajit Singh and Jujhar Singh, the Guru's two surviving sons, fell valiantly fighting sword in hand before his very eyes. Guru Govind Singh with a sweep of his mighty sword cut off the head of Nahar Khan, one of the Mogal generals, and wounded the other, Khwaja Mahomed.

> "Sweeps his long arm-that sabre's whirling sway
> Sheds fast atonement for its first delay."
>
> *Byron.*

But it was a fight against tremendous odds as the Mogals numbered thousands. Dismayed by the fall of their principal commanders, the Mogals momentarily lost hold of their quarry. The Guru and five of his followers, who alone had survived that grim battle, shook off their enemies and rushed into the fort of Chamkaur. But the Mogals came on and besieged the little place. That brave but battered handful of Sikhs could not surely hold out for long in the beleaguered fort. Indeed the situation being altogether desperate, Guru Govind Singh and his companions disguised themselves and gave the slip to the Mogals during the darkness of the night.

The fugitives concealed themselves in a neighbouring forest until dawn broke, when they resumed their flight and soon reached the village of Machhiwara, where the party entered a private garden. Here they were discovered by two Rohilla Pathans,

Ghani Khan and Nabi Khan, the owners of the garden. The Guru who used to purchase horses from the Rohillas in past years was recognised by them. They could have betrayed him to the authorities and earned the rich reward which was set for his capture. For once their minds were assailed by greed, but, after a short mental struggle, Guru Govind Singh's past kindnesses to them weighed down the issue in his favour. Overcome by feelings of gratitude and human sympathy, the Pathans disguised the Guru as a Mahomedan *faqir* and made him out as their spiritual preceptor. They safely conducted him to Behlolpur in Ludhiana district where he found sanctuary with Qazi Pir Mahomed, his old Persian tutor. From there Guru Govind Singh escaped to the waste country around Bhatinda. As these forced flights and constant alarms had begun to tell on his iron constitution, the Guru halted for some days in the village of Raipur to recoup his broken health. As soon as he had regained his normal strength, he proceeded to Muktesar and sent out a clarion call to his followers who had since become widely scattered. More than twenty thousand stalwart Sikhs assembled under the Guru's banners at this place. The governor of Sirhind was alarmed on receipt of this news and despatched a strong force to oust the Guru from his new stronghold.

A bloody battle took place on the outskirts of the town, in which victory shone on the Sikh banners. Guru Govind Singh ordered a tank to be built, called Muktesar, in memory of his brave soldiers who laid down their lives on this battlefield.

It appears that after this the Guru was no more molested by the Mogals. This is mainly due to the fact that he slackened his active hostility to the Mogal government. But another and more significant reason is that the grand army of the empire, which Aurangzeb had led in person to the Deccan to conquer the Marathas, had by now been worn down. In fact it was being beaten back and the aged emperor was enormously worried by the abject failure of his grand undertaking. Intrigues for the succession were already afoot in the North and every Mogal grandee of note was more concerned in securing his personal interests than in tackling the foes of the empire.

Guru Govind Singh proceeded to Malwa preaching the gospel of Sikhism and gained thousands of proselytes. At Damdama near Bhatinda he engaged himself in composing the *Dasam granth.* The emperor, whose mind was ill at ease, far down in the Deccan, on account of the Guru's volcanic activities and expanding influence in the Punjab, invited him to the Deccan, swearing by the Koran to treat him honourably. Probably this was just a device to draw him away from the midst of his great political labours, as it appears unlikely that Aurangzeb should have so suddenly contracted an affection for his quandom enemy at the fag end of his life. Whether it was a genuine invitation or a crafty move on the part of the Mogal, it failed to evoke the desired response. Guru Govind Singh composed a Persian poem of 1400 stanzas, in reply to the emperor, in which he narrated all the barbarous cruelties which the Mogals had inflicted on his family, that the Khalsa would one day wreak vengeance on their oppressors and that personally he knew not fear. By the time the Guru's messenger Bhai Daya Singh reached the Deccan with this reply, Aurangzeb lay on his death bed and passed away in February 1707.

His successor, the emperor Bahadur Shah, desiring to conciliate Guru Govind Singh, sent him a fresh invitation, which was accepted. On reaching the Deccan, the Guru was treated with marked distinction and respect. His bleeding heart could not, however, be healed by this late exhibition of kindness. He left the imperial court and visited a number of places in the Deccan. During these journeys one of his Pathan employees, a horse dealer, grew insolent, at which Guru Govind Singh, being unable to control his wrath, struck off the man's head. Moved by remorse, however, he sent for the dead man's wife and two sons and gave them valuable presents. One day the young men stealthily entered the Guru's resting place and stabbed him to avenge their father's death. While running away they were caught by the Sikhs and brought before the Guru, who nobly forgave them and had them set at liberty. His wound was sewed up. He expressed an ardent desire to see Banda a famous *bairagi* who lived at Nader and was reputed to have performed wonderful penances. Accordingly Guru Govind Singh journeyed to Nader and met Banda, a hill Rajput from Poonch in the Punjab, who, prior to his taking holy orders, had been a great hunter in his earlier days. The magnetic personality of the Guru cast its irresistible spell on Banda and he was initiated into the Sikh faith. His Rajput blood began to boil in his veins as he listened to the horrible tale of Mogal atrocities from the lips of the Guru. At last having been convinced of his warlike antecedents and spirited character, the Guru exhorted Banda to assume command of the Khalsa after he was no more, avenge their wrongs and uproot the Mogal power in the Punjab. The burning enthusiasm of the great Guru had so thoroughly fired the soul of the Rajput devotee that he readily discarded the ochre-coloured robes of the recluse and girded on the sword, buckler, bow and arrows. The Guru gave him five arrows out of his own quiver as an omen of victory. One day Guru Govind Singh tried to bend a huge bow and in so doing burst open his wound which had not yet healed. A spout of blood gushed out. He felt the end approaching. His dying behest to the Sikhs was to obey Banda as their leader, to go back to the Punjab to complete his work, to stick fast to their faith and to look upon the Granth Sahib as their true Guru in future. Then, on the banks of the ancient Godavri, in 1708, the last of the holy Gurus closed his eyes in eternal sleep.

They say that the blood of martyrs is the seed of nations. Such seeds were profusely sown by the Sikh Gurus, their children and innumerable disciples. If they smilingly sacrificed their lives, it was to break the ignoble spell of a ruthless despotism and to lay the foundations of freedom for posterity. What finer tribute can there be to the success of the Gurus than that a meek people whose spirit was effectually crushed by ages of political servitude and who were habituated to put up with every conceivable form of oppression in a spirit of sullen resignation, should be completely transformed into a race of magnificent soldiers. It is a phenomenon of extraordinary political significance. The fact is that the mass of the people, including the sturdy Jat peasantry, were goaded into desperation by the continual persecution and rapacity of the Mogals. It was natural therefore that they should have hailed the advent of the later Gurus, whose spirited message of salvation struck a singularly welcome note in the hearts of the oppressed people. Held together by secret association in the earlier stages they openly took to rapine and plunder later on. Daring Sikh freebooters, well mounted and armed, scoured the country in all directions in search of plunder; their successes meant the development of the Guru's material resources. The latent flame of Sikhism exalted the endeavours and ambitions of the populace. They shed their rich life blood on the plains of the Central Punjab; nor were their sacrifices in vain. That the Great Mogal was not invincible in war inspite of all his military pomp and pride of empire-resources, was the priceless knowledge which the Khalsa had gained. And in the dauntless spirit of sacrifice which pervaded the rank and file among the Khalsa, lay the true secret of their ultimate success. Guru Govind Singh more than made good his famous words that he would so transform the sparrows as to make them kill the hawks in future.

# Chapter X.

# Suraj Mal.

> ......The prize can but belong
> To him whose valour o'er his tribe prevails;
> In life the victory only crowns the strong—
> He who is feeble fails."
>
> *Schiller.*

The rapid rise of Jat power at the threshhold of the 18th century was quite in consonance with the *portentous military developments in* Rajasthan, the Deccan, Bundelkhand and the Punjab, during the last quarter of the previous century, which spelt the widespread disruption of the Mogal empire.

Relying on the loosened bonds of the empire, political as well as moral, petty Jat chiefs openly took to freebooting in the country between Delhi and Agra. They looted imperial treasure and tribute, remitted by provincial satraps, as boldly as merchant's caravens on the high roads converging upon the capital cities. The accumulation of wealth by means of these marauding excursions provided them with the sinews of power and opened out larger vistas of ambition, which was fanned to flame by the weakened authority of the imperial government and its inextricable commitments in the other theatres of war. The Jats' plundering operations were carried on so vigorously in 1691 as to necessitate the despatch of a Mogal expedition against them from Delhi. Under their intrepid chief, Churaman-the lord of Sansani, the Jats, however, proved to be a hard nut to crack. They could never be altogether suppressed. If their depredations ceased in one region, they broke out in another. The Jats forcibly levied black-mail for safe conduct through their territories. The intestine wars among the weak successors of Aurangzeb and the consequent anarchy gave a powerful impetus to their freebooting activities.

Before long their gruff warrior chief raised the banner of independence. The Mogals, alreaby distracted by the rising waves of Maratha encroachment, were severely startled by the audacity of the new power which had sprung up almost under the shadow of the imperial capital. A force was accordingly despatched under Maharajah Jai Singh of Amber in 1720 to reduce the Jats to submission. Unable to meet the foe in open battle, the Jats shut themselves in their strong mud fortresses and baffled all the attempts of the besiegers to capture these strongholds for more than an year. An accommodation was then arrived at, which left the Jats in undisturbed possession of their castles and lands on the stipulation that they would abstain from further aggression and pay a nominal tribute.

Soon afterwards Badan Singh invoked the help of Maharajah Jai Singh to avenge a disgrace which he had suffered at the hands of his cousin Churaman. A short spell of fighting ensued at the end of which Churaman fled from the scene in 1722, leaving Badan Singh without a rival as ruler of the Jats. The court of Delhi was, at this time, torn by factions and intrigues owing to the machinations of the Sayyad Brothers. Under the circumstances it was just natural for the Jat chief to extend his own interests at the cost of the Mogals. And as the years rolled by, the Jat power waxed stronger.

About the close of the year 1731, Badan Singh retired into the seclusion of a religious life after entrusting his eldest son, the celebrated Suraj Mal, with the cares of the state. This patriarchal resolution turned out to be an inestimable boon to the Jat race. Suraj Mal was not only a formidable warrior but he was also richly endowed by nature with quick intelligence and a sound sense of statecraft. One of his kinsmen named Khem Karan, who held the castle of Bharatpur, was disposed to be insolent and defiant towards the young chief. Terrible retribution followed. Suraj Mal stormed the castle in 1733, slew Khem Karan and razed the fortifications to the ground. This vigorous action cowed down other malcontents as well and enhanced the reputation of Suraj Mal among his warlike clansmen. On the ruins of the destroyed castle he laid the founndations of the present magnificent fort of Bharatpur with its broad and deep moat, masonry ramparts, bastions, bridges and temples. It took two decades to build the new fort.

Suraj Mal maintained cordial ralations with his neighbour Siwai Jai Singh of Amber. In 1742, the latter decided to celebrate an *Aswamedh yagya* but as his two sons Ishri Singh and Madho Singh quarrelled and became recalcitrant, the young Suraj Mal was invited to Jaipur to perform the filial ceremonies. The rich gifts which the Maharajah bestowed on his Jat godson on this auspicious occassion enabled the latter to build the present fort of Deeg.

The death of the royal astronomer of Amber next year, led to a war of succession between his sons. Suraj Mal espoused the cause of the elder brother, Ishri Singh, while the cause of Madho Singh was taken up by the Maharana of Udaipur and Malhar Rao Holkar. The powerful aid of the Jats enabled Ishri Singh to emerge triumphant in this tussle of strength. Madho Singh was defeated by

Suraj Mal in the battles of Rajmahal, Begru Kalan and Moti Dungari and for a time disappeared from the scene. The policy of active intervention in foreign politics, formed the keynote of Suraj Mal's subsequent career. He gave a vigorous direction to the martial activities of the Jats. His eagle eyes were constantly fixed on the fluctuating fortunes of court intrigue at Delhi, which he exploited to his best possible advantage. He abetted hostile movements and formed alliances as it suited his own designs.

In 1745 the emperor Ahmad Shah ordered Asad Khan, an imperial general, to attack the Nawab of Kol ( Aligarh ) who had withheld certain revenues. The latter sought the aid of the Jats in his hour of distress. Suraj Mal gladly took up the side of the Nawab and marched to his succour at the head of a strong force. A battle was fought near Aligarh in which Asad Khan was slain and the Mogals were utterly routed. Large quantities of war stores fell into the hands of the victorious Jats. To avenge this disgrace, the emperor deputed Saadat Khan, the Amir-ul-Umara, in 1748, to lay waste the Bharatpur territories. Suraj Mal made elaborate preparations to meet the danger. Before long the clash took place at Naugaon in which the Mogals were again defeated in pitched battle. This was the second time that the Jats under their gallant ruler, had worsted the arrogant Mogals in open battle and the moral advantages of these successes proved to be extremely valuable to the former. The emperor was deeply impressed with the fighting power of the young Jat state and finally gave up the attempt to subdue it.

Ahmad Khan Bangash, the Pathan Nawab of Farrukhabad, broke out into revolt in 1749. The Nawab Vazir was therefore authorised by the emperor to form an alliance with Holkar and Suraj Mal in order to chastise the rebels. The allied army came up with the rebels at Shamsabad Mau where a fierce action took place. In hand to hand fighting, Suraj Mal slew Rustam Khan, a prominent leader of the Pathans, who broke and fled. All the ten districts of the Pathan chief were overrun and partitioned among the confederacy, a big slice of fertile country falling to the share of Suraj Mal.

Mogal power and prestige had waned to such a degree that Wazir Khan, a Mew robber, had established a regular reign of terror in the Mewat country about the year 1730. The emperor was flooded with complaints and appeals for protection from the depradations of this wily robber, who commanded a gang of one thousand desperadoes, all armed to the teeth. It almost appeared as if Wazir Khan would also set up an independent dynasty of his own in the close proximity of Delhi. He had bravely beaten back several Mogal detachments which had been sent out to suppress him. It was not easy to catch him up as his movements were incredibly swift and elusive. At last his activities became so alarming that a formal Darbar was convened at Delhi in which the emperor called for a volunteer to extirpate the dreaded robber chieftain. None of the Mogal grandees was eager to take up the gauntlet. The silence of the Darbar hall was, however, broken by Bir Bahadur Singh, a guest of the emperor. He stood up, drew out his sword and declared that it would not re-enter the sheath until it had severed the head of the outlaw. This bold volunteer was a Birgoojar Rajput of gigantic proportions. The emperor was immensely pleased and promised to appoint the daring Rajput as ruler of the Mewat country as soon as the outlaw was slain. Bir Bahadur Singh set out on his dangerous mission at the head of one hundred chosen horsemen.

The party had covered a distance of 20 miles south of Delhi when news arrived that Wazir Khan, with 500 followers laden with booty, was about to cross the Jumna into Alwar territory. Loath to let their quarry escape, the Rajputs charged sword in hand. A deadly conflict ensued in the *bela* of the Jumna, and within an hour the keen Rajput blades had done their destructive work. Wazir Khan though covered all over with wounds, fought grimly to the end; his followers were unable to stand the shock and fled. His head was soon cut off and brought as a present to the emperor. This exploit gained to Bir Bahadur Singh all the rich rewards which had been promised and the title of Rao. He established his capital at Ghasera near Gurgaon and for 20 years ruled over the turbulent Mewat country with an iron hand. By steady encroachments the Rao extended his territory until in 1750 it touched the north western confines of the Jat kingdom.

Suraj Mal was alarmed and desired to come to an amicable understanding with the Rao about their mutual frontier. Accordingly a couple of months prior to the Ganges bathing festival in 1751, Suraj Mal met him at Palwal. As the Rao was inclined to be haughty, the unfortunate meeting ended in a fiasco. Suraj Mal had dissembled his real feelings and came away with rage gnawing at his heart. He lost no time in persuading his quondam ally and friend Mansur Ali Khan, the Nawab Vazir, to get him the emperor's sanction to attack the unsuspecting Rao. As in previous years, the devout Rao proceeded to the Ganges at festival time but on his way back he learnt that all the principal fords of the Jumna were guarded by Jat pickets and shrewdly concluded that the Jats were lying in wait for him. He escaped to Delhi in disguise and made his way to Ghasera without further misadventure. Outwitted at the passage of the Jumna, Suraj Mal forthwith assailed his enemy's country and one fine morning the Rao awoke to the dreadful din of war drums. He peered out of his palace window and found that his citadel was besieged by the Bharatpur army. Little did he imagine that the feud would so soon recoil on his head like a fearful thunderbolt.

There was a mere handful of Rajputs within the fort. The valiant Rao clothed himself in saffron robes and, accompanied by his only son and a small band of retainers, sallied out of the fort. But the odds were overwhelming and physical valour was of little avail against trained musketry. The fight was bloody but brief. The besiegers had for the moment to give way before the concentrated fury of the Rajput attack. However the Rao and his son had soon received numerous wounds; a musket ball pierced the forehead of the former. Both having been mortally wounded were carried into the fort and the two Ranis of the dying Rajput chief committed *sati* there and then amid the fading din of the unequal battle. Thus was a whole noble family, with its dependents, blotted out of the roll of existence within a few hours.

"In small proportions we just beauty see;
And in short measures life may perfect be."

*Ben Jonson.*

Maharajah Ishri Singh of Amber died during the same year and was succeeded by his younger brother Madho Sing who bore an implacable enmity towards the Jats, ever since his forced flight from Amber in 1743. Two years later Mansur Ali Khan fell into court disgrace and had to fly from the capital. Suraj Mal joined him with 15000 Jat cavalry at Faridabad and marched on Delhi to overawe the emperor. Ghazi-ud-din, the Mogal general, came out with a large army to contest the progress of the daring foe. However the Jat leader and his warrior son, Jawahir Singh, captured the Mogal artillery at Arab Sarai by a swift attack and drove the Mogals almost right up to the walls of Delhi. The Jats plundered the suburbs, killing thousands of the people who showed resistance. Tales are still told in Shahdara, then a large and flourishing grain market, of the thoroughness with which the town was sacked by the Jat soldiery. Roofs were pulled down, walls were ripped open and floors were dug up by the Jats in their hunt for gold and silver bullion. On the arrival of fresh Mogal reinforcements the fortune of war shifted. Sharp actions were fought at Badarpur, Faridabad and Ballabgarh, in all of which the

Jats were worsted. Flushed with these successes, Ghazi-ud-din became overbearing in his conduct towards his compeers and this brought him almost to the verge of downfall.

Suraj Mal was of course always on the lookout to exploit rival ambitions at the Mogal court. He persuaded Intizam-ud-dowla, who was getting jealous of Ghazi-ud-din's influence, to secure a pardon from the emperor for Mansur Ali Khan. The trick succeeded and the Khan was ordered to resume his viceroyalty. Suraj Mal was also ingratiated into the royal favour again, to such an extent that the emperor wrote him a secret letter suggesting a plan to outwit Ghazi-ud-din. As luck would have it, the letter fell into the hands of the latter. He was exasperated beyond measure and openly charged the emperor with duplicity. Suraj Mal realised only too well that the tell-tale letter had raised a storm of which he would have to bear the full brunt. Ghazi-ud-din had a large and well equipped army at his command and determined to wreak his vengeance on Suraj Mal. Accordingly in 1754, he formed a league with Madho Singh of Amber and Malhar Rao Holkar, the old foes of the Jats, and burst upon the Bharatpur country. It was a critical time for the Jat state but it was saved by the consummate military abilities and tenacious resistance of Suraj Mal. In the open field, Ghazi-ud-din was met with guerilla tactics while the forts, which bristled all over the country, belched forth fiery defiance at him in whatever direction he turned. A stray shot in the siege of Kumbher, near Deeg, killed Khande Rao, the husband of the celebrated Ahalya Bai and the only son of Malhar Rao Holkar, who got disgusted and left the country. Before long the mercenary invaders, having paid a heavy toll of life without gaining any appreciable advantage, became weary of the war and began to withdraw. The enraged Jats fell upon the retreating Mogals with a vengeance and soon drove them out of the country.

A rebellion of Jat chiefs, headed by Bhure Singh, broke out in the year 1757. The rebels unfurled the flag of independence and started on a plundering expedition in the Gangetic Doab. Suraj Mal promptly scotched the rebellion before it could assume dangerous proportions and captured the fort of Mursan, the rebel headquarters.

Meanwhile Ghazi-ud-din made his way to the capital and re-organized his party. The emperor, who was fidgetting under his insidious yoke, was ruthlessly murdered on 30th November 1759, and Shah Jahan the Second was raised to the throne. These infamous proceedings, however, raised a powerful opposition at court; the consequence was that Ghazi-ud-din soon found himself a fugitive and sought the protection of Suraj Mal.

Although his erstwhile foe, the Jat ruler was too shrewd a diplomat to refuse asylum to such an influential personage. At this time the Maratha pressure on Hindustan was squeezing the life out of what remained of the broken Mogal empire. Their very name was a terror to the court of Delhi and to the Nawab Vazir of Oudh. At last the Mogals in their despair invited Ahmad Shah Abdali, the Afghan king, to deliver them from the Maratha menace. Malhar Rao Holkar was busy consolidating Maratha supremacy in the north. A large Maratha army under the Peishwa's son arrived in 1758 to reinforce Holker. Suraj Mal and Ghazi-ud-din joined it on the Betwa river and marched on Delhi, which lay prostrate before them. For a time, however, the crisis was averted by the successful negotiations of Suraj Mal, which resulted in the recognition of Shah Alam as emperor and the Marathas withdrew from Delhi. Ghazi-ud-din now sank into oblivion; he passed the remainder of his life at Kam Pahari under Jat protection.

Events were now fast leading up to the third battle of Panipat. Suraj Mal naturally rallied under the Maratha banners with an auxiliary force of

30000 men. He advised Rao Bhao to wear down the *Moslem host by ceaseless guerilla war*. As this wise counsel was treated with undisguised contempt, Suraj Mal left the field in disgust. Although the Jats did not participate in the battle, yet they rendered yeomen's services to the thousands of Maratha fugitives who poured into their country after the battle was over. Bhao fell fighting on the battlefield but his widow and half-brother, Shamsher Bahadur, the son of Baji Rao by his Mahomedan wife Mastani, repaired to Bharatpur and were treated with all the consideration due to their exalted rank. The lady was escorted to Maharashtra and the remains of Shamsher Bahadur, who died of his wounds, were interred in a tomb at Bharatpur, near which a mosque was also erected by the orders of Suraj Mal. All other fugitives were hospitably treated and supplied with money to enable them to return to the Deccan.

With the departure of Ahmad Shah Abdali, for Kabul, the country sank into anarchy again. Suraj Mal was quick to take advantage of the situation. He swooped down on Agra and captured the fort with all its accumulated treasures since Akbar's reign. The splendid mausoleum at Sikandra did not also escape the victor's attentions. Suraj Mal stripped it of all the precious jewels with which the walls of the inner tombs were inlaid. His eldest son Jawahir Singh conquered fresh territories towards Alwar and in the north, which were added to the Bharatpur dominions. By the close of 1761, Suraj Mal had more than doubled his kingdom by fresh conquest. The districts of Agra, Muttra, Aligarh, Rohtak and Gurgaon were wrested from the feeble hands of the Mogals and formally annexed. It appears that Suraj Mal was converging upon Delhi from various directions and there is little reason to doubt that, had he lived long enough, he would have succeeded in his cherished design of capturing the imperial capital.

The Jats had reached the zenith of their glory at this time. The sack of Agra and its environs placed fabulous riches at the disposal of Suraj Mal. Amidst the rugged pursuit of war, he now found time to adorn his capital with handsome public buildings and temples. In particular he built the famous fountain palaces of Deeg, which, Thornton says, "are surpassed in India for elegance of design and perfection of workmanship only by the Taj Mahal."

In November 1763, Sumroo entered the service of Suraj Mal with a powerful park of artillery, a trained Sepoy brigade and a number of European adventurers. On this fresh acquisition of armed strength, Suraj Mal considered it time enough to make a bold bid for the possession of Delhi, the nearest goal of his ambitions. As a matter of fact a dangerous sore had appeared in the palm of his hand, which the physicians declared would soon prove fatal. It is highly probable that this fact also induced him to undertake a glorious campaign which might be likely to prove his last one. A pretext was faked up to commence hostilities. He laid claims to the military command of the capital, which he knew the Mogals would never willingly concede, and simultaneously began the march on Delhi. Before the Mogals were fully aware of his bold designs, Suraj Mal had seized Rewari, Bahadurgarh and Farrukhnagar. The vast riches of Kamgar Khan, the *jagirdar* of Farrukhnagar, were plundered. Even Shahdara was occupied by the Jat forces. There was consternation within the capital and had luck shone on the standards of Suraj Mal, he could without much difficulty have coerced the puppet emperor of Delhi into granting his demands. But the cup of Suraj Mal's life was now full to the brim. He started with a slender escort to reconnoitre in the *bela* of the Jumna, where the whole party was surprised by a large Mogal squadron under Said Khan Baloch. The Jats were asked to surrender. This they haughtily rejected and bravely fell fighting to a man. Thus did the greatest of the Jat rulers meet a soldier's death early in 1764, while battling with his foes under the walls of Delhi.

Jawahir Singh, who lay encamped in Farrukhnagar, proceeded to Deeg and ascended the *gaddee* in January 1764. When he presented himself before his mother Maharani Kishoree for her blessings, she taunted him for having come away from the battle-ground without avenging his father's death. The youthful warrior solemnly swore to wreak vengeance on the Mogals as desired by the dowager Maharani. He enlisted powerful detachments of Maratha and Sikh auxiliaries and before a couple of years had elapsed, was in full march on Delhi. The city was besieged for six months and during this period the suburbs as well as a part of the city viz. Sabzi Mandi and Naya Bans, were plundered. Eventually peace was concluded with the Mogals at the intercession of his ally Holkar in February 1766.

# Chapter XI.

# Madhoji Scindia.

"Dreams of a peaceful day,
Let him dream who may;
'War' is our rallying cry,
Onward to victory."

*Treitschke.*

"Strike, strike at the trunk of the withering tree and the branches will fall of themselves. By directing our efforts to Hindustan, the Maratha flag, in your reign, shall fly from the Krishna to the Attock," urged the youthful Peishwa Baji Rao in impassioned tones. His tall handsome person, ringing voice and fiery eloquence held the Maratha Cabinet spellbound in silent admiration. The Maharajah Sahu could no longer resist this noble rhetoric and exclaimed "By God you shall plant it on the Himalayas !" If Baji Rao had the vision to look ahead and plan for the future, he had the strength and vigour to execute as well. Having silenced the opposition of his critics at home, he singled out with unerring judgment the finest military captains of Maharashtra to carry out his bold designs on the tottering Mogal empire. While Pilaji Gaekwar bore down on Gujrat, Ranoji Scindia, Malhar Rao Holkar and Udaji Powar were sent off to invade Malwa. The Mogal army under Khan-i-Dauran could not possibly roll back the rising tide of Maratha invasion. On the conquest of Malwa by the combined armies of Scindia, Holkar and Powar, Baji Rao parcelled out the country between them into three *jagirs*. The northern *jagir* was bestowed on Ranoji Scindia, who established his capital at Ujjain.

The comtemporary Mogal emperor at this time, Mahomed Shah *Rangila,* was entirely given to licentious pursuits and merry-makings, of which a fair idea can be formed by the fact that he had in effect given up the reins of power in the hands of his favourite eunuch Jawed Khan, a sexless *Hijra,* and Adham Bai, a prostitute, better known as Qudsia Begum. While Mahomed Shah was content to beguile his time in the palace in wild revelry in the company of his low class favourites, the court was being torn to peices by fierce jealousies and dissensions among the Persian and Turkoman nobles. Such was the state of affairs at Delhi when, in 1736, the Marathas under Baji Rao invaded Hindustan. Ranoji Scindia took a distinguished part in this campaign. At the time of his death in 1747, the annual ravenue from his Malwa domains amounted to about Rupees sixty five lakhs.

He left six sons behind him, viz. Jayapa, Dattaji, Jotiva, Santaji, Madhoji and Tukoji. These young men were all born warriors and fought with distinction on many a far-flung battlefield in the interests of the expanding Maratha empire. Jayapa and Santaji laid down their lives in 1754 while battling in Marwar; Jotiva was killed in a battle in Bundelkhand; Dattaji was killed in the Punjab in a brush with the Afghans. As a matter of fact the Marathas were swarming up from the Deccan under daring leaders in the endeavour to uproot the effete empire of the Mogals. Keene says "The heart of the exhausted empire had now almost ceased to beat......The ruin of the government had been gradual and soon it became final." Balaji Baji Rao, the 3rd Peishwa, determined at this stage to deliver a knockout blow at the empire in order to realise the dream of Chhatrapati Shivaji and to complete the labours of Baji Rao, his predecessor in office. Accordingly a powerful Maratha army marched on Hindustan under the supreme command of Sadasheo Rao Bhao and Vishwas Rao, the Peishwa's brother and son respectively. It was joined by the forces of the principal feudatories of the Maratha empire.

Scindia's forces were led by Jankoji, the son of Dattaji, and he was accompanied by his uncles Madhoji and Tukoji. Eventually in 1761 the Maratha and Afghan hosts lay facing each other on the battlefield of Panipat. It is needless to relate here the various blunders on the part of the Maratha generals which weakened their tactical position day by day, gave mortal offence to powerful chiefs like Holkar and Suraj Mal and before long resulted in a crushing defeat of the Maratha army. Seeing that all was lost, Sadasheo Rao and Vishwas Rao charged into the thickest of the battle and were seen no more.

Madhoji Scindia had witnessed the fall of his nephew and brother; the fatal battle had turned into a rout. Had he too thrown away his life, it would have served no useful purpose whatsoever. Accordingly Madhoji mingled himself in the stream of fugitives and escaped from the battlefield. He rode a magnificent Deccani horse which however excited the cupidity of a gigantic Afghan trooper, who started in pursuit. It was now a race for dear life. Wounded and bleeding, Madhoji was no match for his burly enemy. Unfortunately Madhoji's horse failed to clear a ditch and came down with its rider to the ground. The Afghan rushed up, rifled Scindia's valuables and rode off on his horse, leaving Scindia lying in the ditch for dead. As he lay there groaning with the pain of his wounds, a Mahomedan water carrier, named Rana Khan, who happened to pass by, took compassion on the sufferer and brought him out. Rana Khan seated Madhoji on his bullock and took him to a village near by, where the wounds were dressed. After a few days he safely conducted Scindia to the Deccan.

Born in 1732, Madhoji had already seen active service before the battle of Panipat in the Deccan wars of 1754. He never forgot the lasting debt of gratitude he owed to Rana Khan, who had been instrumental in saving his life and easily persuaded him to enter his service. Throughout the rest of his life Scindia used to address Rana Khan as *Bhai*, meaning brother. Basking in the sunshine of Scindia's favour, Rana Khan, the humble water-carrier, developed into a successful military officer as was amply proved in the later wars. On his arrival at Poona, young Madhoji was welcomed by the Peishwa Madho Rao, who conceived a genuine affection for him. The question of the family *jagir* now cropped up and the Peishwa, inspite of a good deal of opposition from his uncle Raghoba, decided to confer it on Madhoji Scindia. Malwa had passed out of Maratha hands after the disaster of Panipat. The Peishwa directed Madhoji Scindia to invade the country and bring it back under the Maratha yoke. Accordingly Scindia took the field in 1765 and not only overran the whole of Malwa but several other tracts of Central India simultaneously, thereby regaining his family *jagir* and adding fresh territory to it.

The star of Madhoji's great destiny was now steadily rising. His reconquest of Malwa won him greater honour and esteem at the court of Poona. By 1768, the Marathas had recuperated the loss sustained by them in the last battle of Panipat, and the Peishwa resolved to invade Hindustan again to re-habilitate the prestige of Maratha arms. Prior to his departure from Delhi, Ahmad Shah Abdali had appointed Najib-ud-Dowlah, a Rohilla Afghan, as Amir-ul-Umara to carry on the Mogal government. It was indeed the successful diplomacy of Najib which had created a strong Mahomedan league against the Marathas before the battle of Panipat. For this reason the Marathas harboured a powerful craving for revenge against Najib and Rohilkhand. In 1768, the Peishwa despatched an army under Visaji Krishna to invade Hindustan and avenge the disaster of Panipat; it was soon augmented by the forces of Madhoji Scindia and Malhar Rao Holkar. The Maratha host now proceeded to Rajputana and levied heavy arrears of tribute from the Rajput princes who were unable to resist. They next bore

Madhoji Scindia

down on Bharatpur and secured an even bigger haul from this state. At this time the emperor Shah Alam was away in Allahabad while the government was being run from Delhi by Najib-ud-Dowlah. The near approach of the irresistible Maratha army, which was cantoned at Deeg owing to the outbreak of the monsoon, so terrified Najib that he sought peace on humiliating terms. Madhoji Scindia was strongly opposed to this proposal which he considered to be a device of the Rohilla chief to escape the fearful retribution in store for him, now that the country was in the grip of the Maratha armies. Holkar on the contrary desired to accommodate Najib. As there was thus a serious difference of opinion in the Maratha camp, Visaji Krishna referred the matter to Poona for decision. Meanwhile Najib humbly came to the Maratha camp, placed his son Zabita Khan under the protection of Holkar and left for Najibabad, the town lately founded by him, where he died in 1770. On receipt of orders from Poona, the Marathas avenged Panipat by carrying fire and sword through the Gangetic Doab, and a part of Rohilkhand. This country was reduced to shambles and all the accumulated hoards of Najib were plundered.

Najib was succeeded at Delhi by his son Zabita Khan who possessed neither the talents nor the courage of his father. All that he cared for was license and revelry. He outraged the chastity of the ladies of the royal palace; his followers committed similar misdeeds in the city of Delhi. The people grew sick of their crimes; the grandees of the court became equally disgusted. Maratha emissaries meanwhile proceeded to Allahabad where the emperor was living under British tutelage, and excited his interest to such an extent that he began to pine for return to the glorious capital of his race. He opened secret negotiations with the Marathas, through his trusted councillor Hissam-ud-Dowlah, for restoration to the throne of Delhi. Shah Alam agreed to pay Rupees ten lakhs to the Marathas on the accomplishment of this design and came over to Farrukhabad for the purpose. There he was met by Madhoji Scindia who took him under his protection and carried him over to Delhi on 25th December 1771. This brilliant coup altogether upset the far sighted plans of Warren Hastings for the extension of British influence westwards.

Zabita Khan fled from Delhi on Scindia's triumphant entry leaving behind him a large part of his father's wealth as well as his family. These riches fell into the hands of Madhoji who ordered Ghulam Qadir, the son of Zabita Khan, to be secured and confined in Delhi. The Mogal court was now such a storm centre of intrigue that the political kaliedoscope was changing with amazing rapidity almost from day to day. The Nawab Vazir had returned to Delhi and was feverishly working in collusion with the Rohillas and the weak-willed emperor to set up a strong alliance to oust the Marathas from the capital. Madhoji Scindia got an inkling of these plots and was quite pleased at the prospect of an open war to finally settle the question of political supremacy over Hindustan. He was a deadly enemy of the house of Najib, whom premature death had saved from Maratha vengeance. Scindia put in a strong plea to carry the issue by force of arms but Holkar and the other Maratha chiefs favoured the gentler path of diplomacy. Zabita Khan was really playing a double game all along. While professing his solicitude for the aims of the Nawab Vazir, he was simultaneously carrying on secret correspondence with the Marathas among whom he counted Holkar as a strong friend. These plots and counter plots resulted in an agreement between the Marathas and Zabita Khan which secured the office of Amir-ul-Umara to the Rohilla and the fertile plains of the Gangetic Doab to the Marathas. Madhoji Scindia was thoroughly displeased with this bargain as in his opinion the Marathas had let slip a golden opportunity to win the permanent ascendency over the lifeless empire of Delhi. Being too shrewd and patriotic a diplomat, however, to quarrel with his confederates over this issue, he left at the head of his army for Jaipur.

News was suddenly received from Poona, in November 1772, of the death of the Peishwa Madho Rao and Scindia therefore left for the Deccan. The deceased Peishwa having left no son, the court raised his younger brother Narayan Rao to the Peishwa's *gaddce*; this gave mortal umbrage to his scheming uncle Raghoba, who coveted that high office for himself. Raghoba was undoubtedly the stormy petrel of Maratha politics. His machinations and foul intrigues totally upset the equilibrium of the Poona court and in 1773 led to the murder of the minor Peishwa. The partizans of Raghoba now elected him Peishwa and with a view to conciliate public opinion, which was incensed at the brutal murder of Narayan Rao, advised him to go to war with the Nizam and Haidar Ali. The majority of the Maratha Sardars were however not to be circumvented so cheaply. They lodged Narayan Rao's widow, who was pregnant, in a place of safety, where she gave birth to a posthumous son named Madho Rao Narayan. No sooner that Raghoba had marched out of Poona, a silent revolution took place in the city and the infant son of the murdered Peishwa was formally proclaimed as the rightful successor to the *gaddee.* Raghoba was bitterly stung at being thus outwitted; he gave up his pretext of war and headed for Poona to contest his claims. However he was opposed and defeated by a detáchment of Madhoji Scindia's army under Haripal Phalke. Barred from entering Poona, Raghoba fled to Surat and sought British help.

The dissensions in the Poona cabinet emboldened the foes of the Maratha Commonwealth to take up the offensive and tear off strips of Maratha territory. Haider Ali crossed the border and began to ravage the country by his depredations. The ruler of Kolhapur tore off a large slice from the Peishwa's territories. Although Rao Bhao had died fighting on the battlefield of Panipat, yet an impostor secured possession of the Konkans in his name. The Nizam also took up an aggressive attitude. These dangerous movements, which started simultaneously in distant parts of the Peishwa's dominions, brought home the gravity of the crisis to the Poona statesmen, who thereupon deputed Madhoji Scindia to safeguard their territorial interests against hostile interlopers. To start with, Scindia overpowered the resistance of the pretender who had possessed himself of the Konkans and took him prisoner. The Raja of Kolhapur was next attacked and not only forced to restore the territory seized by him but to pay a war indemnity of Rs 15 lakhs in addition. Madhoji then turned round and came to grips with Haider Ali, who was badly defeated and obliged to pay a heavy indemnity; and the Nizam was dealt with as effectively. While Madhoji Scindia was delivering these swift strokes to humble the Peishwa's enemies, the partizans of Raghoba made a last bold bid in Poona to secure their master's designs. The conspirators had planned to capture Nana Farnavis but he got scent in the nick of time and escaped to the fort of Purandhar. Madhoji Scindia hastened to Poona to nip the evil in the bud and completely frustrated the designs of the malcontents who fled from the scene. Nana Farnavis was brought back to Poona and entrusted with the high office of chief secretary to the Peishwa.

Raghoba had since entered into a treaty with the Bombay government at Surat, stipulating to cede Bassein and Salsette on condition that the British helped him to ascend the *gaddee* of the Peishwa. This led to the outbreak of the 1st Maratha War. As soon as the Bengal government came to know the details of the treaty of Surat and that the war was undertaken to advance the personal interests of an unpopular pretender like Raghoba, they entered into a fresh treaty with the Poona Cabinet at Purandhar in 1776 and put a stop to the war condemning it as 'impolitic, dangerous, unauthorised and unjust'. Madhoji Scindia paid a visit to his Northern possessions about this time and, as the Jats had created some trouble, overran the Bharatpur State. He was not disposed to restore the country, so conquered by force of arms, but, be it said to his eternal credit, on the intercession of the dowager Maharani, the widowed mother of Jawahir Singh, he forthwith restored the country and returned to the Deccan where matters of grave political concern were transpiring.

England was on the eve of war with France. Nana Farnavis had shown marked courtesy to St. Lubin, a French emissary, who had brought valuable presents to Poona from the French emperor. Accordingly the Court of Directors resented this hostile display; they repudiated the treaty of Purandhar and ratified the treaty of Surat. War with the Marathas was now inevitable. Raghoba's party in Poona led by Sakharam Bapu were inspired by fresh hopes of success; they won over Holkar to their side which led to the temporary discomfiture of Nana Farnavis, the staunch supporter of the infant Peishwa's claims. Madhoji Scindia descended on Poona on hearing of these sinister developments and rudely pricked the bubble of Raghoba's inordinate desires. Sakharam was taken prisoner and met his doom for treason at the hands of Nana Farnavis; Holkar left the field to his opponents and returned to Indore. A British army had since started from Bombay to instal Raghoba on the *gaddee* at Poona. Scindia marched out to give battle and drove back the Bombay army, which began a disastrous retreat. It was soon enveloped on all sides by the Marathas and, in 1779, forced to sign the humiliating Convention of Wargaum, which enabled the British force to save itself from a desperate situation. In Keene's words "The commanding officer fell sick; the military member of council lost his head; the column was hemmed in and cowed into retreat; officers and men became demoralized; the stores were burned, the guns thrown into a pond." But the Convention was repudiated by the British government and war was resumed. Colonel Goddard penetrated the heart of Gujrat but was utterly confounded to find himself surrounded on all sides by the mobile forces of Madhoji Scindia and Tukoji Rao Holkar; all the allurements of Warren Hastings to detach Holkar from the Maratha confederacy had proved futile. The Colonel was in a hopeless quandry; he was stuck in the heart of a hostile country and was unable to effect a retreat. The war was thus going unfavourably for the British when Major Popham was despatched from the side of Bengal to attack Malwa in order to create a diversion. Keene says that "the war in fact was becoming a duel between Scindia and Warren Hastings and for some twelve months the ablest men in India faced each other in earnest conflict." Major Popham won over the Rana of Gohud and assailed the fort of Gwalior although it was reputed to be impregnable and General Sir Eyre Coote characterised it as a mad attempt. For more than two months the British army tried in vain to capture the fort. On the 3rd August 1780, Captain Bruce and a picked body of soldiers scaled the walls of the fort at dead of night, with pads tied to the soles of their feet, so as to deaden all sound, and after a sharp hand to hand fighting overcame the resistance of the surprised garrison. The escalade was carried out under the leadership of a dacoit who had volunteered to guide Captain Bruce up the frowning rock at the western base of the fort.

The sudden fall of the fort of Gwalior retrieved the previous military reverses of the British government to a considerable degree. It was, as a matter of fact, more anxious for peace at this time than the Marathas whose concentration was increasing in every theatre of the war, whereas the British treasuries at Calcutta and Bombay had been practically emptied. It was this fact which soon after drove Warren Hastings into those questionable proceedings against Raja Chet Singh, Nand Kumar and the Begums of Oudh which finally ended in his miserable and long drawn out trial in England. Peace was concluded between the British government and Madhoji Scindia with the result that all his territories south and west of the Jumna were restored to him on 13th October 1781. The fort of Gwalior was however made over to Rana Lokinder Singh of Gohud as a reward for his friendly cooperation with the British during the late war. The famous treaty of Salbai was negotiated in the following year mainly through the clever diplomacy of Madhoji Scindia who stood surety for its observance on behalf of the Poona Court and thereby secured the lion's share of advantages.

The Rana of Gohud was found guilty of treachery by the British government in 1783 and was given up to the wrath of Madhoji Scindia with whom cordial relations had been inaugurated by the treaty of Salbai. The fort of Gwalior was therefore attacked by Scindia's forces under De Boigne; but all attempts to take it by storm or escalade were stoutly repulsed. De Boigne had then recourse to strategem. He bought over Moti Ram, an influential officer among the garrison, who secretly admitted the besiegers into the fort. As soon as the brave Rani of Gohud, who was within the fort, learnt of this treachery, she ordered her faithful attendents to set fire to her apartments. The leaping flames and crackling debris soon told Scindia's army how the noble lady and her maids had perished rather than court the ignominy of capture. Gohud was simultaneously reduced. Soon after Rana Chutter Singh was himself captured at Karoba and lodged as a state prisoner in the fort of Gwalior, where he died in 1785. By the close of the year 1783, the victorious armies of Madhoji Scindia had taken Bhind, Sikarwari and Sabalgarh; the conquered territory was permanently annexed to his dominions in Central India. Appaji Khande Rao and De Boigne invaded Bundelkhand and levied the inevitable *Chouth* from a number of states.

It is evident that the diffusion and versatility of Scindia's armies at this period made them practically irresistible to the other native rulers in India. This high level of efficiency and power was by no means the result of any accident. On the contrary it was the natural outcome of the incomparable military talents and strenuous endeavours of Madhoji Scindia. In the background of his lofty political ambitions stood his army-well equipped, disciplined and strong. Having discerned the vast superiority of trained battalions over irregular troops, a gifted leader like Scindia could not but put a high premium on the value of European military discipline. Madhoji Scindia entrusted the task of drilling his armies to a number of French officers, among whom De Boigne, a native of Savoy, occupies the foremost place of honour. From his boyhood upwards, De Boigne had passed his whole life in camps and wars and was one of the best exponents of the European art of war. He won his generous master's unqualified admiration by the splendid account which his trained battalions gave of themselves in numerous wars. Scindia was so pleased as to raise De Boigne's salary from Rs. 1000/- to Rs. 10000/- per mensem within a short time. That Scindia's confidence and royal munificence were not ill bestowed is fully borne out by the fact that his armies of the new model held practically the whole of Northern India at bay and were a terror to hostile principalities.

Here is another instance of Scindias' magnanimous liberality. After the sack of Delhi by Nadir Shah in 1738, the Indian branch of the Bourbon family had managed to escape from Delhi with a part of their movable riches. They took sanctuary in the fort of Asirgarh, within the family *jagir*, which had been conferred on them by the emperor Akbar. In 1778, the Raja of Narwar, within whose territories the *jagir* was situate, was so enraged at the insolence of Francis Bourbon, the head of the family, as to order the massacre of all the male-members and attacked the fort which was defended by Francis. There being no hope of success against the Raja's forces, the small band of defenders sallied out under the command of Francis and his son Salvador Bourbon. They all perished with the exception of Salvador's son, bearing the same name, his mother and some younger children, who made good their escape to Gwalior. Madhoji Scindia was so moved by compassion on the sad plight of the distinguished fugitives as to bestow on them two villages in *jagir* in his own dominions and a large house for their residence in Gwalior. Soon afterwards Salvador, acting on his mother's counsel, left for Bhopal and joined the service of the Begum Mumola. On the Begum's death in 1792, he was driven back to Gwalior to seek refuge; but four years later Salvador Bourbon furnished a signal proof of base ingratitude towards his benefactor's interests. He fought as commander of the Bhopal forces against Scindia's army which was led by Mon. John Baptist Fanthome and succeeded in narrowly averting the fall of the fort of Bhopal.

On the close of war with the British, Scindia had not only obtained honourable terms but had largely extended his territorial interests. He was now free to devote all his attentions to the shifting politics of the imperial court, where, he knew, as if by instinct, that his brilliant genius could find full scope for its natural expression. With a powerful army at his beck and call, there was no obstacle which could long stand on the highroad of Scindia's exalted destiny. The Mogal court was hopelessly distracted by assassinations and intrigues. The emperor was little better than a puppet in the hands of unscrupulous nobles and his authority existed only in name. On the death of Mirza Najaf in 1782, a scramble ensued between his sons and nephew for distribution of his wealth aud succession to the office of Amir-ul-Umara. Afrasiyab Khan, a son of the Mirza, had assumed the office but his self-constituted authority was challenged by other claimants and appeared unlikely to last long. In order to put an end to these terrible feuds, which hung like a thunderclap on the head of the hapless emperor, he invited Madhoji to the capital to settle the issue. This was a welcome opportunity which Scindia could not sensibly let go. He marched on Agra where the emperor came to see him. The rival claimants for the office of Amir-ul-Umara also waited on Madhoji Scindia and each tried to enlist his sympathies in his own cause. While these diplomatic conversations were being carried on in Agra, Afrasiyab Khan was one dav found murdered; it is alleged that the murder was committed at the instigation of Scindia. This allegation has apparently found credence by the fact that Shah Alam, whose nerves were racked by a series of political murders, now sought the protection of Madhoji Scindia and conferred on him the disputed office. The latter politely declined to accept it for himself but secured it for the Peishwa and consented to act on his behalf. This diplomatic action has been variously interpreted by historians. Some believe that his loyalty to the Peishwa was genuine and that he ardently desired to augment the power and prestige of the Maratha confederacy, in whose efficiency he had full faith. According to other critics, Scindia was at this stage intent on founding a powerful kingdom for himself, that his consideration for the Peishwa meant nothing in effect and that it was merely a ruse to hoodwink the Marathas and the British about his real designs on Hindustan. Probably the truth lies midway. As the power of the Peishwa had declined, there was no need for Scindia to propitiate Poona out of any possible fears. It follows that Scindia did not repudiate the Peishwa out of sheer patriotic motives. Again it is difficult to understand why Scindia should have declined to take over the proffered administration of the Mogal empire. Towering above the prevailing degeneracy and decay, the Maratha warrior-statesman, daring, strong and full of resource, would have been more than human if he had thrown away the tempting prize.

The Mogal army was placed under Scindia's command and to meet its expenses, the revenues of the districts of Agra and Delhi were assigned to him except that a small sum was reserved for the private and palace expenses of the imperial household. To watch over his new interests, Madhoji Scindia brought over his capital to Muttra, so as to be within striking distance of Delhi. He was now the virtual ruler of the empire of Delhi. He administered the country, collected tribute from the Jat and Rajput States and called upon defaulters to pay up arrears. The Mogal governors of provinces were asked to render proper accounts. Though treated with respect, the emperor was confined in Scindia's camp in Muttra where he was closely guarded. Madhoji Scindia called upon the British government also to yeild the annual tribute for the provinces of Bengal and Behar but this demand was refused on the ground that it was contrary to the terms of the treaty of Salbai. In 1785 he was visited by Mr Malet, the British Agent at the court of Poona, who was put up by Scindia's orders in the Taj Mahal at Agra, where the British Resident lived.

The proud Rajputs were severely piqued by the revolutionary change which had installed Madhoji Scindia into the seat of supreme power at Delhi and resented his demand for tribute. Accordingly the rulers of Jaipur and Udaipur made common cause and lent their aid to the Rajputs of Raghogarh who were battling against Scindia's army. The Mahomedan nobles of the court were also disaffected and sowed the seeds of disloyalty among the Mahomedan officers of Scindia's army with the result that when the latter marched on Jaipur to suppress the Rajput revolt, a part of his forces under Mahomedan officers suddenly deserted and went over to the Rajputs. Scindia was compelled to effect a retreat to Gwalior. On receipt of fresh reinforcements however he marched on Agra and relieved his general Lukwa Dada who was besieged in the fort. Madhoji Scindia now proceeded to his camp in Muttra to watch the trend of affairs at Delhi where scenes of unparalleled horror were about to be enacted.

After Scindia had turned his back on Muttra, the emperor Shah Alam was not allowed to remain there much longer. He was persuaded to distrust the Marathas and leave their protection. The old man was spirited away to Delhi in this mood by his new set of advisers. He had however soon cause to lament this hasty action. Zabita Khan having died in 1785, he was succeeded in the family estates by his son Ghulam Qadir who captured Delhi with a small force and, posing as the champion of the Mahomedan nobility, demanded money from Shah Alam to turn out the Marathas. The emperor swore that he did not possess enough money to meet the demand of the young Rohilla but failed to convince him. Fearing violence he appealed to Scindia to extricate him out of the sorry predicament. But the latter remained unmoved in Muttra, inexhorable as fate. He could not possibly realise the extent of the peril which confronted the emperor and deliberately allowed matters to drift so that the old man should learn a sharp lesson at the hands of the Mahomedan nobility and thus put an end to his vaccilating imbecilities for good. Getting wind of these secret negotiations, Ghulam Qadir summoned the emperor in July 1788 and again pressed his demand for money. Threats and abuses could not however fill an empty treasury. The emperor pathetically denied the existence of the alleged secret hoards of wealth which the Rohilla wanted him to disclose. Finding that words had failed to produce any effect, Ghulam Qadir had the hapless emperor flogged in his presence by prince Bedar Bakht, the heir to the throne. The Begums of the royal seraglio were next assaulted and flogged without the least respect for their sex or exalted rank. The monster was still far from being satisfied in his mad quest for hidden treasures. He finally summoned all the members of the royal family on 10th August 1788 and threatened them with terrible punishment if his demand was not instantaneously met. Shah Alam bowed his hoary head in meek resignation at the frightful indignities which were heaped upon him. The Begums were beaten before his eyes; their jewellery was violently torn from their tender bodies; and the climax of these inhuman barbarities was reached when Ghulam Qadir gouged out the eyes of the aged emperor with his own dagger and trampled them under his feet. He was about to mete out the same treatment to the royal princes but desisted at the passionate entreaties of Shital Das Jain the royal treasurer.

Delhi was paralysed with horror and apprehension on receipt of this news which quickly fled to Muttra and caused a furore in the Maratha camp. Madhoji Scindia was rudely startled at the audacity of the Rohilla adventurers who had perpetrated these heart-rending atrocities on the royal family. Sharp orders were therefore issued to Rana Khan, Ladoji Shitole, De Boigne and Madhoji Phalke to march to Delhi to apprehend Ghulam Qadir and deliver his royal victims. Alarmed at the approach of powerful divisions of the Maratha army, Ghulam Qadir fled, with all his spoils of the royal palace, towards Meerutt. The Marathas took possession of Delhi and set free Shah Alam and his ladies from their misery. It is easier to imagine than to describe the fervent blessings which the blind emperor and the tearful princesses showered on Madhoji Scindia, who had thus delivered them from the clutches of their fiendish persecutors. In fact Shah Alam composed a poem to depict his condition at the time, the melancholy pathos of which is enough to melt the stoniest human heart.

Scindia issued fresh orders that Ghulam Qadir must not be allowed to escape. Accordingly Rana Khan started in pursuit and captured the fugitive at a distance of 7 miles from Meerutt. On being produced before Scindia, Ghulam Qadir was asked to explain why he had committed such brutal excesses. As the prisoner took up an attitude of brazen insolence, Scindia ordered his tongue to be drawn out. His eyes were next taken out and his hands and feet were cut oft. The living wreck of Ghulam Qadir was then sent off to be thrown at the feet of the blind emperor, by way of atonement. But the Maratha soldiery hanged the human wreck while on the road to Delhi and carried the dead body before Shah Alam.

After Nemesis had thus overtaken Ghulam Qadir, and Delhi was relieved from its anguished suspense of the past two months, Scindia started for Delhi. A wave of delirious joy swept over the capital on his coming. He reseated Shah Alam on the throne of his ancestors, sanctioned a pension of Rs 5 lakhs per annum for him and bestowed *jagirs* and other rich rewards on deserving Maratha officers. The imperial capital, the emperor and the empire now lay prostrate at Madhoji Scindia's feet. After all he had achieved the great dream of dominion over Hindustan which he had conceived in 1769 at the time of the first forward drive of the Marathas after Panipat. Within twenty years of that fateful movement Madhoji Scindia had fought down his rivals, overcome stupendous obstacles and outwitted the Mahomedan nobility of the Mogal empire at their own game of statecraft. Shah Alam having recovered the pageant of his defunct empire conferred the title of 'Madar-ul-Miham Alijah Bahadur' on his protector.

Now that affairs at Delhi were satisfactorily settled, Madhoji Scindia found time to visit the Deccan. The Peishwa accorded him a royal reception as Scindia had all along scrupulously maintained his prestige at a high level. In a public darbar at Poona, Scindia presented the Peishwa with the titles and robes of honour which had been secured for him from the puppet emperor of Delhi. Scindia's magnificent successes in Hindustan and his consequent influence with the Peishwa were an eyesore to Nana Farnavis, who tried to bring him into disgrace. But these ignoble attempts were foredoomed to failure; his machinations were unable to shake the implicit confidence which the Peishwa reposed in his exalted guest. On 12th February 1794, Madhoji Scindia quietly passed away in the village of Banori, situated at a distance of three miles from Poona.

The achievement of Madhoji Scindia represents the high water mark of Maratha paramountcy over Hindustan. "A soldier and statesman of almost unsurpassed ability", he was for close upon a quarter of a century the biggest actor in Maratha and Mogal politics. There is no wonder that he was looked upon as the sole prop of the tottering thrones of Poona and Delhi.

> "As some proud column, though alone,
> Thy strength had propp'd the tottering throne."
>
> *Scott.*

Like all great men he was the personification of his times and contemporary history is largely reflected in his great overland marches between the Deccan and the North, his brilliant efforts to maintain the power of the Maratha confederacy and his wars with the British, the Rajputs and the Mogal nobility. With consummate intelligence he frustrated the designs of Raghoba, who tried to break up the Maratha confederacy in order to advance his personal interests. Later on, Madhoji Scindia again overreached the British diplomats by securing the dependence of the emperor Shah Alam, who repudiated his obligations to the British and fled from Allahabad to seek Scindia's protection. Colonel Malleson observes "It must never be lost sight of that the great dream of Madhoji Scindia's life was to unite all the native powers of India in one great confederacy against the English. In this respect he was the most far-sighted statesman that India has ever produced. It was a grand idea capable of realisation by Madhoji, but by him alone, and which, but for his death, would have been realised."

# Chapter XII.

# Yashwant Rao Holkar.

"Pride in their port, defiance in their eye,
I see the lords of human kind pass by."

*Goldsmith.*

Yashwant Rao Holkar was one of the four sons of Tukoji Rao Holkar, the adopted son of the illustrious Ahalya Bai. On the death of Tukoji Rao in 1797, his legitimate son Kashi Rao Holkar was raised to the throne of Indore; but the succession was disputed by his younger brother, Malhar Rao. The rival claimants appealed to Nana Farnavis for arbitration and proceeded to Poona for the award. While there, Malhar Rao was killed by treachery. Yashwant Rao fled to Nagpur to save himself but found his way back to Malwa within a few months after meeting with various adventures. He now pretended to espouse the cause of Khande Rao, son of the late Malhar Rao, and began to collect a nondescript army of Marathas, Rajputs, Bhils and

Pindaris in his name. After a chequered course of desultory fighting he succeeded in driving out Kashi Rao and seized the throne of Indore for himself. A couple of French soldiers of fortune, Duderneque and Plumet, who held important commands in Kashi Rao's army, deserted their master on his discomfiture and took service under the successful Holkar. They proved very useful to him in his subsequent wars. Other petty chiefs also joined him with their quotas, of whom a notable one was Amir Khan with his troop of Rohilla freelances.

Central India presented a scene of extraordinary turmoil and war at the close of the 18th century, due to the jarring interests of the great Maratha leaders who held sway therein. Each wanted to grab as much territory as he could at the expense of his neighbour. The atmosphere was charged with plot and counterplot. The country swarmed with raiders of every race possessing tender mercies, who were driven by the insatiable thirst for plunder Human life was held cheap; riches were unstable. To make headway in the midst of such wild tumult a leader should not only possess ample physical strength but also clear brains, an iron will and the ability to strike swiftly. Yashwant Rao was richly endowed with these virtues. The tale of his career is almost an unbroken record of war and military

Yashwant Rao Holkar.

adventure which casts a lurid light on the stormy nature of contemporary politics.

As soon as he came to power in 1798, he began to strike out. The title of Nawab and several rich gifts were bestowed on Amir Khan and he was sent off to raid eastwards. In fact Holkar could not gain power except by resorting to the law of force and plunder. As a famous French general once put it, offence is the best form of defence; and the instinct of self-preservation alone was a strong impulse in Holkar at this period. He had good reason to be careful of his powerful neighbour Scindia. The whole of Malwa was parcelled out between Holkar and Scindia and large tracts of the country were often changing hands owing to the clash of their rival ambitions. A veritable hell of fighting, loot and arson broke loose on the country on the heels of Amir Khan's raid and Daulat Rao Scindia lost a considerable slice of his territories. He was then staying in Poona as the guest of the Peishwa but soon hurried towards the north with a large army to invade Malwa. Yashwant Rao met him in the open field. Although he hurled back Scindia's army in an earlier engagement, yet, he lost the day at Satwas and was forced to retreat. Holkar did not however take long to recoup his strength and, as the monsoon broke, his army was in full march on Ujjain, the capital of Scindia. A tough battle was fought outside the walls of the city which left Yashwant Rao undisputed master of the field. The city was spared the horrors of a general pillage on payment of a large ransom.

To avenge this disgrace Scindia despatched a well equippd army under Sirje Rao Ghatge, after the rains, to invade Indore. Yashwant Rao marched out from Ujjain in all haste to save his capital and stood at bay to await Scindia's onset. The battle lasted for ten days in which the arms of Scindia finally triumphed. Indore now lay at the mercy of the conqueror and suffered the same fate as had befallen Ujjain. Yashwant Rao retreated with the remnants of his shattered force to Jamghat. The waning star of his destiny was however to soon shine forth with renewed lustre.

Hardly a couple of months had elapsed since his retreat from Indore when Holkar decided to attack Rutlam. With the swiftness of a hawk he covered a distance of 80 miles on horseback in a single day and suddenly presented himself before the amazed town. There was consternation on every face and very little resistance worth the name. Yashwant Rao secured a rich haul from the town and leisurely proceeded to Maheshwar. In 1801 he despatched an army under Fateh Singh Mane, one of his most trusted generals, to attack the territories of Scindia and the Peishwa, while with a larger army he himself marched north and ravaged a host of towns in Rajputana. Zalim Singh the able Regent of Kotah saved his capital by paying a cash *nazar* of seven lakhs of rupees to the irresistible invader.

After similar depredations Holkar turned back in 1802, with an army numbering 1,44,000, and proposed to Scindia and the Peishwa that he would like the latter to act as mediator between him and Scindia to bring about an amicable settlement. This was merely a ruse. He had old scores to settle against both of them and they seem to have been hoodwinked by the crafty proposal. Holkar marched right up to Poona without being molested. They discovered their blunder when Yashwant Rao was thundering at the gates of Poona. Baji Rao, the Peishwa, ordered one of Holkar's brothers to be tied to the foot of an elephant and dragged through the streets of Poona until he was killed. The bloody battle of Poona in October 1802 sealed the fate of Baji Rao, and his dynasty for ever. Holkar won a complete victory over the allied armies of his foes. Baji Rao fled to the port of Bassein, about twenty miles to the north of Bombay, and sought the protection of the British government; it resulted in the well known treaty of Bassein on 31st December 1802. Meanwhile

Yashwant Rao was having things his own way at Poona where he remained at ease for three months and wanted to raise the son of Amrit Rao to the *gaddee* of the Peishwa. But this plan remained unfulfilled as a large British army was advancing on Poona to reinstal Baji Rao. Since Yashwant Rao was not in the mood to enter into a futile war with the British he started back for Malwa. But by the time he reached home, he had sacked numerous towns in the Nizam's territories which lay in his line of march and exacted a heavy tribute from Aurangabad.

The treaty of Bassein had laid the axe at the roots of the political and military organization of the Maratha empire in Hindustan. By one stroke of his diplomatic genius Lord Wellesly had practically secured the dismemberment of the Maratha Commonwealth. But Scindia and Bhonsla were not prepared to take it lying down without striking a blow for the vanishing glory of the Maratha nation. They repudiated the Treaty, provoking thereby the Second Maratha War and invited Holkar to join them in fighting the British. Yashwant Rao was at first inclined to join them and terms were mutually agreed upon for united action. But he drew back at the last moment considering that it would be more advantageous for him to leisurely ravage the northern provinces while Scindia and the British were fighting each other out. He also wanted to watch the issue of the great struggle. Eventually the treaties of Arjungaon and Devgaon, at the end of 1803, put an end to this war.

Yashwant Rao Holkar now remained the only great power in India who had not yet acknowledged the supremacy of the British. He was ill pleased with their victories in the recent Maratha wars and with a view to form an irresistible confederacy against them he started secret negotiations with Scindia, the Bundelas, Jats and Sikhs. Each of these rising powers had cause for alarm at the all-embracing political designs of Lord Wellesly who had not only crumpled up the Peishwa's temporal power but had already caught the weaker dynasts of India in the far flung meshes of his Subsidiary System. Out of the blue ocean a great power had sprung on the shores of this country to champion the cause of the weak and to evolve stable government from the prevailing strife and racial antagonisms.

Early in 1804 Holkar launched a powerful expedition to invade Hindustan. While levying *Chouth* from the Rajputana states he urged them to shake off the British yoke which they had recently imposed upon themselves. These provocative proceedings and hostile negotiations were being narrowly watched by the British Government.

On being warned by the Governor General to desist from his predatory activities among the protected states, Yashwant Rao boldly claimed it as his right to collect *Chouth* as before and to compel defaulters to pay him by force of arms. Both parties were now rushing into the vortex of the Third Maratha War and, in April 1804, the British Government decided to strike the first blow before the union of their foes could materialise.

Colonel Monson penetrated into Malwa from the north and captured the forts of Rampura and Hinglasgarh, which seem to have been abandoned by Yashwant Rao. Though in command of a large army and a strong park of field artillery, the wily Maratha was really luring on the British commander into the interior. From the south west Colonel Murray was marching through Gujrat to effect a junction with Monson's army. The war was a regular tussle of wits and military strategy between the combatant generals. Yashwant Rao was a Maratha warrior of the old national type, distinguished by rapid strokes and daring expedients. He avoided pitched battles until he had made sure of success. He luckily succeeded in enlisting the sympathies of Bapoo Scindia, a nobleman of Gwalior, who commanded a cavalry force under Monson. By western theatre of war cut off Colonel Murray's supplies and soon drove back his force into Gujrat.

Meanwhile Monson had passed through the Mokundra Pass, having been joined by Rajput contingents sent by the rulers of Kotah and Jaipur to aid the British Government. A cavalry force under Lieutenant Lucan, which had ventured too far from the main body of Monson's army, was cut to pieces and Lucan was taken prisoner. Monson now received the disconcerting intelligence that Holkar had turned back and was bearing down on him at the head of an overwhelming host. A general retreat was therefore ordered to get out of the trap. To protect the rear of the British army, a small force, including the Rajput contingents, was stationed near the Mokundra Pass. It gallantly bore the terrible shock of the Maratha attack at the Ford of Amjar and was practically destroyed. Yashwant Rao had retaken the forts of Rampura and Hinglasgarh and now started in hot pursuit of Monson's army. It was ceaselessly harried by day and night attacks until it degenerated into a flying rabble and trickled into Agra about the end of August 1804. Monson lost five complete battalions and six companies during the disastrous retreat.

This triumph served to brighten up Maratha prospects as well as to ruin British prestige in

Hindustan. Ranjit Singh, the Jat ruler of Bharatpur, repudiated his alliance with the British and openly threw in his lot with Holkar. The latter now took possession of Muttra. General Lake came up to oppose Holkar and skirmishing took place for several days between them. Holkar rushed upon Delhi which was successfully defended by a small force under Ochterlony. Failing to capture Delhi, Yashwant Rao marched to Shamli and Farrukhabad where heavy cavalry fighting took place. Forced to fall back he proceeded to Deeg to join the Jats. He safely deposited his guns within the fort of Bharatpur and began to lay waste the Gangetic Doab. General Lake, however, soon drove Holkar back to Deeg and captured the fortress though after considerable sacrifices. Yashwant Rao took refuge in the fort of Bharatpur, which was besieged by the British from January to April 1805. During this period four heavy attacks were launched on the fort but were repulsed every time by the garrison with conspicuous success.

The struggle had been a very ding dong and undecisive one: both sides were feeling exhausted by this time. The rainy season had set in and brought about a temporary cessation of hostilities. Yashwant Rao returned to Malwa unmolested by the British. The term of Lord Wellesly as Governor General was over and he was succeeded by Lord Cornwallis, who, dying within three months of his arrival, was again succeeded by Sir George Barlow. The East India Company was tired of the recent wars which had absorbed all their profits and ill approved of the apparently unremunerative imperial projects of Lord Wellesly. The Governor General was accordingly directed by the Court of Directors to make immediate peace with Holkar and meddle no more in the affairs of Indian rulers. Yashwant Rao thus lost very little by the war and practically emerged triumphant. The other great Maratha leaders regretted the Subsidiary treaties into which they had entered, imposing all sorts of drastic restrictions on their liberties. Scindia openly joined Holkar. Some of the Rajput rulers also shook off the trammels of the Subsidiary System.

After the rains of 1805, Yashwant Rao again invaded Hindustan with a huge army. He levied contributions from numerous Rajput states. From Jaipur alone he secured 18 lakhs of rupees, as the British declined to interfere in pursuance of the new policy. As the sphere of Holkar's depredations increased and the political interests of the Company were consequently placed in serious jeopardy, the Governor General could not at last afford to remain inactive. General Lake was therefore despatched in pursuit of Holkar into the Punjab in order to reduce him into submission. Eventually a treaty of peace was concluded with him by Sir John Malcolm on the 24th December 1805 on the bank of the Beas River.

In 1808 Yashwant Rao exhibited symptoms of insanity and slid into the background of Maratha politics. The disease steadily developed. He died on the 28th October 1811. A fine *Samadh* and statue stand in his memory in Bhanpura, Indore State.

Yashwant Rao was a man of middle stature possessing an extremely powerful and muscular frame. He lost the sight of his right eye while target shooting in 1798 but this accident, rather than diminish his martial ardour, served only to whet it. In horsemanship and the use of arms he was matchless. He was a true Maratha of the old school, always preferring guerilla warfare over pitched battles in the open field and provokingly swift and elusive; these tactics seriously confounded the English generals in the Third Maratha War. By his daring and personal prowess he had come to be reckoned as one of the most intrepid military captains of his age. The martial races of Central India and Hindustan looked upon Yashwant Rao as a hero. Colonel Sleeman mentions that Yashwant Rao's name was successfully invoked from the Nerbudda to the Indus by those who suffered from ague and fever which left them immediately. Sleeman himself shook oft the fever like this, though he says he was "certainly no lover...of...Yashwant Rao Holkar." A strange phenomenon, the authenticity of which cannot be doubted, based as it is on such a high authority.

Yashwant Rao's army always presented a most picturesque spectacle, being composed of soldiers belonging to heterogeneous races-Marathas, Rajputs, Pathans, Jats and Sikhs. In fact adventurers from every part of India flocked to serve under his banners. He was as clever an organizer as he was skilful in war. Whenever there was respite from actual war, sham fights were held twice a day in which the great war lord personally went round to inspect the conduct of his meanest soldier, approving, criticizing, scolding. No wonder then that the army intensely loved him. The various branches of the army were organized on a sound military basis. Huge founderies were built which cast cannon and turned out all types of smaller arms. As a military strategist he ranks among the foremost generals who have ever trod on Indian soil. His heroic achievements shed a noble lustre on his military genius, political sagacity and indefatiguable industry. He was undoubtedly the greatest and most romantic figure on the stage of Indian history during the opening decade of the 19th century.

> "The greatest gift the heroe leaves his race
> Is to have been a heroe.............
> We feed the high tradition of the world,
> And leave our spirit in our children's breasts."
>
> *George Eliot.*

# EPILOGUE.

"And we will pray that from their clay
Full many a race may start,
Of true men, like you men,
To act as brave a part."

Our hallowed memories spontaneously evoke John Ingram's fervent prayer! The endless roll of our heroes could not possibly be compressed in a handy and popular volume like this. I am keenly conscious of the paucity of my effort and I much wish I could embrace the theme in fuller measure. However I have deliberately refrained, due to various considerations, from adding to the matter and bulk of this volume.

In 'Heroes aud Heroe Worship', Carlyle says "Yes....................in all times and places, the Heroe has been worshipped. It will ever be so. We all love great men; love, venerate and bow down submissive before great men: nay can we honestly bow down to anything else? Ah, does not every true man feel that he is himself made higher by doing reverence to what is really above him? No nobler or more blessed feeling dwells in man's heart. And to me it is very cheering to consider that no sceptical logic, or general triviality, insincerity and aridity of any Time and its influences can destroy this noble inborn loyalty and worship that is in man. In times of unbelief, which soon have to become times of revolution, much down-rushing, sorrowful decay and ruin is visible to everybody. For myself in these days, I seem to see in this indestructibility of Heroe worship the everlasting adamant lower than which the confused wreck of revolutionary things cannot fall. The confused wreck of things crumbling and even crashing and tumbling all round us in these revolutionary ages will get down so far; no farther. It is an eternal corner stone, from which they can begin to build themselves up again. That man, in some sense or other, worships Heroes; that we all of us reverence and must ever reverence Great Men; this is to me, the living rock in all rushings-down whatsoever;—the one fixed point in modern revolutionary history. otherwise as if bottomless and shoreless."

The prophetic utterances of Carlyle have been amply borne out by lessons from history, times out of number. The very sentiment of hero-worship is ingrained in human blood. And in nourishing this sublime sentiment lies the salvation of any people.

## III

Peace came in the wake of British supremacy in India over a hundred years ago. Raging torrents of armed men no longer disturb the tranquility of our battle-scarred countrysides. The spirit of the West, with all its exhuberance of energy, enterprise, industry and scientific development, has completely galvanized the life of the Orient: the sleeping Princess has awakened. Modern civilization is today impinging hard on our ancient culture, customs, morals and manners. We have faced the blast fair and square; and made it subserve the desire for all-round development. That the pace of progress has been lately accelerated is evidenced by the fact that we have produced orators, thinkers, scientists and statesmen of international repute during the past quarter of a century.

The fact that Hinduism converges in the blood of people of heterogeneous races is no argument for the diversity of their interests, nor can dialectic or territorial differences be held to mark out lines of cleavage of the nation. It is therefore worth our while to retain our distinct individuality, not in any bellicose spirit towards any other section of our fellow-countrymen, but in a spirit of mutual esteem and broad good will towards all, which is indeed one of the noblest principles of Hinduism. If we hold fast, with unimpaired faith, to our true cultural moorings, we could never go down in the fiercest struggle for existence. That "the very foundation of the whole commonwealth is the proper bringing up of the young" was a basic truth stated by Cicero. The problem of national education is one of the close concerns of the State in western countries and is treated as a science as well as an art. Victor Hugo once remarked that "He who opens a school, closes a prison"; and the Duke of Urbino, who founded one of the greatest of Italian libraries, ruled that "every book should be bound in crimson, ornamented with silver." It must be remembered, however, that simultaneously with the powerful advocacy of learning in the West, the aspirations and impulses of its youth are never allowed to drift into capricious channels. For example the average British boy scout, strapping, self-reliant and strong, is well versed in the exploits of the celebrated heroes of Great Britain-navigators, sailors, soldiers and explorers; he longs to emulate their noble passions.

"The soul, aspiring, pants its source to mount."

*R. Montgomery.*

In short the education of our youth is a sacred trust which rests heavily on the shoulders of the Hindu leaders of the age. It is up to them to direct the national effort into the proper channels, so as to co-ordinate and organize the whole. James

V

Allen observes "To put away aimlessness and weakness, and to begin to think with purpose, is to enter the ranks of those strong ones, who only recognise failure as one of the pathways to attainment; who make all conditions serve them and who think strongly, attempt fearlessly and accomplish masterfully." A touch of Rousseau and a stronger touch of Lieutenant General Lord Baden Powell in the methods of education of our youth, complemented with earnest efforts to inculcate the spirit of reverence for our heroes, would immeasurably help to build up a healthy and vigorous manhood of the nation.

"Ponder well and know the right;
Onward the and know thy might."

*Goethe.*